Paul Bullinger is a lifelong angler and nature lover. His love for fishing began by spending time as a young boy with his friends in rural Essex, catching crucian carp from a small pond. Paul and the same friends still fish and laugh together years later. Paul is married to Linda and has two sons from a previous marriage and three stepchildren. He lives just outside Norwich.

Dedicated to Uncle "Corks" who introduced me to fishing, the "Bens" whose friendship is so very precious to me, and my wonderful wife, Linda, who persuaded me to finish writing this book.

Paul Bullinger

# REELING BACK THE YEARS

AUSTIN MACAULEY PUBLISHERS™

LONDON • CAMBRIDGE • NEW YORK • SHARJAH

A CIP catalogue record for this title is available from the British Library.

ISBN 9781035826223 (Paperback)
ISBN 9781035826230 (ePub e-book)

www.austinmacauley.com

First Published 2023
Austin Macauley Publishers Ltd®
1 Canada Square
Canary Wharf
London
E14 5AA

Cover photo of the author fishing the Wye was taken by Laurie Platt. Thanks to him.

I would like to thank Austin Macauley Publishers for the part they played in getting my book printed and published.

*A Holiday Fisherman* by Maurice Headlam.

*Fishing in the Norfolk Broads* by Peter Collins.

# Table of Contents

**An Introduction to the Introduction**　　　　**11**

**Introduction**　　　　**14**

**Part 1**　　　　**19**

Chapter 1: Hutton　　　　21

Chapter 2: Billericay　　　　33

Chapter 3: Still in Billericay　　　　43

Chapter 4: Stock Village　　　　53

Chapter 5: Work & Ilford Connection　　　　57

Chapter 6: The Influence of Gerry　　　　62

Chapter 7: Friendships Grow　　　　80

Chapter 8: Mixing Business with Pleasure　　　　88

**Part 2**　　　　**95**

Chapter 9: Assorted Tales　　　　97

**Part 3**　　　　**119**

Chapter 10: In Pursuit of Barbel　　　　121

Chapter 11: A Change of Scenery　　　　134

Chapter 12: The River Wye                               140

Chapter 13: A Change of Venue                   159

Chapter 14: Of This and That                    185

# An Introduction to the Introduction

I am not the main focus of this book, merely the storyteller. All the recollections involve other characters and I thought it would be useful to put these individuals into some kind of context.

I will concentrate on those friends who collectively are known as "The Bens".

This title was derived from old British slang meaning "yes". The actual phrase was "not many Benny" when asked a question to which the answer would be a "yes", as in 'Do you want a beer?' Answer 'not many Benny.' Those clever ones among you would probably wonder why we didn't just answer "yes". Sadly, I can't answer that for you. Keep pondering.

As with all groups of friends, nicknames began to creep in over the years. Those too are listed below.

Here then is the "glossary" of individuals making up our "gang" all those years ago. They are in no particular order.

An old "business card" lists 10 names alongside the rather fanciful heading "Bens International" with a stylised "thumbs up" drawing. These cards were given out to young ladies in the 1960s who, no doubt, tore them up and binned them the moment our backs were turned.

The names read:

Ray

Al

Colin (Bag)

Mitch

Paul

Pete

Laurie

Dave

Pete (Hoppy)

Colin

A few of these guys wandered off to other pastures over the years, namely Colin (Bag), Mitch and Colin. Dave remains a strong Ben but is not a fisherman, preferring instead cricket and line dancing (not at the same time). Pete (Hoppy) is mentioned in some early escapades but hasn't been fishing with us for some years.

Paul (Baldy): This is me. Born in Hutton, Essex. Moved around quite a bit. Now in Norfolk. Noted for talking the hind legs off a donkey. Never ask me about how a Kelly Kettle works or you'll be stuck listening for hours. Lifelong angler.

Ray: My immediate neighbour when growing up in Hutton. A year older than me. My "blood brother". It was his idea (aged about 8) to each prick a finger and put them together, so we became "blood" brothers. I do not recommend this to anyone! Despite living 100 miles from each other, we are in regular contact. Lifelong angler.

Al: Another neighbour from my Hutton days. Al lived four houses away. Ray and I would gang up on him and throw balls of mud at him when he was in his garden. He still loves us. Lifelong angler.

Laurie (HB): The "HB" could refer to his hairy back, but it doesn't. You can decide what it refers to. Let your imagination run wild. Laurie is part of the Ilford crew. Ex-firefighter. Now lives in Norfolk. Lifelong angler.

Pete (Dad): Part of the Ilford crew. Father figure to us all. Great organisational abilities. Only occasionally loses his temper with us. Lifelong angler.

Andy (Boy): Comparative youngster (still in his 60s) Ray and Andy are brothers-in-law, which is handy. Spent some years working and living in the USA (rumoured it was to get away from Ray) Lifelong angler.

John (Codger): Oldest of The Bens. He is Colin's (Bag) brother-in-law. Proof that "old" and "wise" do not always go hand-in-hand. Lifelong angler.

Ian (Nice Bloke): Sadly, no longer with us. A latecomer to our fishing adventures. A truly lovely bloke. RIP.

Other characters pop up from time to time, but the mainstay of our angling exploits are those listed above.

# Introduction

I don't normally read the "Introduction" section of a book, preferring instead to go straight to Chapter 1 and get into the "meat" of it. However, I would urge you to read this Introduction as it gives a short background on my fishing provenance and the reasons as to why I have penned this work.

I have been fishing, on and off, for over 60 years. It has cemented lifelong friendships, taken me to some wonderful places and given me an appreciation of the natural world. It has taught me patience and tolerance. Other fishermen tend, on the whole, to be similar in outlook.

Despite my lifelong addiction to fishing and the countless hours I have devoted to it, I have to admit that I am not very good at fishing. Sure, I can catch fish in most places but the really large, rod-bending monsters have always eluded me. Quite simply, I lack concentration, which is an important component to any angler's disposition.

My school report once read 'Paul seems to daydream his way through lessons.' It is this daydream syndrome that I blame on my inability to be a fantastic fisherman. Sit me on a river bank and I'll dream my way through my float dipping under the waters' surface, my rod being dragged into the raging River Wye by huge barbel and reservoir trout snapping at my artificial flies.

Anyway, over the years I have realised, like so many fishermen before me, that there is more, much more to fishing than just, well, fishing!

In this book, I hope to explain how fishing can bring people together, make us aware of our surroundings, understand nature, develop both humour and a thick skin, learn how to relax and, quite simply, appreciate everything we have. So, quite a tall order, I'm sure you'll agree, but hey, I'm a fisherman and we live in hope all the time!

As a dear (now sadly departed) fishing friend of mine said as we sat in a boat surrounded by the hills overlooking the magical Lough Caragh in South West Ireland 'Always remember Paul, that catching a fish is a bonus.' How right he was.

When you are in stunning surroundings or even in a modest urban park lake, you will be among plants, insects, birds and all manner of nature's creations. You may be with like-minded people or alone with your thoughts. Whatever the situation you find yourself in, one thing is for sure, if you catch a fish, that is the icing on the cake.

There was a temptation to write this book in chronological order. Indeed, I start by recounting my "Early Years" of fishing whilst growing up in rural Essex. However, it is difficult to place events in a strict order of occurrence; did my first trip to Co. Kerry come before or after my first trip to Wales?

To be honest, it doesn't make any difference to the telling of the tales, so you'll forgive me if I stray away from the correct timeline now and again. You wouldn't know anyway!

Whilst offering these apologies, can I also beg your forgiveness for my poor writing. English was not my strong point at school (see previous comments) and, as a consequence, you will spot many grammatical errors and the odd punctuation faux pas. Unless you are an English teacher or University lecturer, I am sure you will ignore these transgressions and plough on!

So, in this book, I hope to convince you, dear reader, that fishing is more than "a worm at one end and a fool at the other" as once described by Dr Samuel Johnson.

Here it is then, my recounting of how fishing has played an important role in my life. The enjoyment I gain from it, the lifelong friends I have made because of it, the places I have seen and the impact it has made on all aspects of my life.

I am eternally grateful that fishing came into my life.

Since writing this introduction, circa 2010 from memory, it now appears that every man and his dog (not literally), have published a fishing book. There is also a plethora of TV fishing programmes. The books and the TV programmes all feature famous people. Celebrities who have been "closet" anglers for years, it seems. I am not even a minor celebrity.

I did appear in Antiques Roadshow once, standing in the background whilst Tim Wannacot talked to the camera. I also appeared laughing briefly on a TV documentary about the value of old fishing tackle and how collectors/investors were buying old rods and reels hoping their values would increase quicker than bank savings rates (not difficult).

The programme was filmed at Angling Auctions in Hammersmith, where I was a regular buyer, albeit at the "bottom end" of the market. I have no idea what I was laughing at (maybe the ludicrous price of old Hardy reels?), but it did get me on the telly.

So, I am not a celebrity and as such I do not have that "cache" to make you purchase this book, but hopefully, as you have already got this far, you may already have "flashed the cash". Thank you.

# Part 1

# Chapter 1
# Hutton

**The Early Years**

When I was ten years old, a favourite uncle made me a split cane rod with a greenheart top section. Up to then, I had fished with a bamboo stick, one of several my father would use for the runner beans. I would tie nylon line to the end, fix on a balsa wood float (carved from a block of balsa that I bought from a model shop) and put on the hook. No need for split shot in those early days. The lump of bread I used could have sunk a battleship! It was enough to cock the float. And some.

With this early, crude version of a pole, I used to cycle to an old bomb crater near to my home in Hutton, Essex and fish for crucian carp. There I would spend countless days with friends fishing for these little slabs of gold. And I would dream. The sun always shone. It was always warm. The skylarks would rise into the clear blue sky and their song could be heard long after they had almost disappeared and become a tiny dot in the sky. Magical days.

But then Uncle "Corks" made me **the** rod. He once asked my father, 'How can you expect the boy to fish with that?' pointing to my adapted bamboo runner bean fishing pole.

My father ignored him. So it was that whilst staying with my uncle and aunt in Norwich for Christmas in 1961, I was given the split cane rod. Now, let's get one thing straight. Uncle Corks knew what he was doing. He was a director at Taylors' Wood Merchants in Wroxham. He knew about wood and he knew about fishing. Although it was homemade, the rod was better than any rod available in the shops. Why? Because it was made specifically for me. At ten years of age, I had a personalised fishing rod!

Boxing Day found four of us fishing the River Wensum at Thorpe. Uncle Corks, Cousin Andy, father and me. As in all the best stories, only one fish was caught, a 2lb roach by yours truly. On my new rod. I had christened the rod in style. I was truly hooked. Fishing was destined to become a big part of my life from then on.

Imagine my excitement when, as Spring approached, I was able to impress my friends with a proper rod, reel and all. Look out crucians!

Looking back on those days, it was amazing how us young lads managed to survive. When we weren't at school, we were either fishing, tramping over the fields, climbing trees or making a "camp" in the nearby woods. We would scramble over barbed wire fencing, fall in the local river Wid, light fires (having stolen a box of matches from home!) and get up to all kinds of mischief. We were rather like the gang in Richmal Compton's *Just William* books!

I feel quite sorry for today's kids. For the vast majority, they will never know the thrill of climbing to the top of a huge ancient oak tree or the joy of playing in the mud along a riverbank or just laying on a straw bale looking up to the sky whilst chewing on a bit of straw "Huckleberry Finn" style.

I'm not convinced that sitting in a darkened bedroom playing on a Xbox with imaginary friends is conducive to a healthy lifestyle for a young child.

Uncle Corks continued to play a pivotal role in my development as a young fisherman. Holidays were often spent with my aunt and uncle because, as they lived in Norwich, we could go to the wonderful Norfolk coast and play on the sandy beaches at Great Yarmouth and Gorleston.

However, my uncle was also a very adept beach fisherman. We would travel to Sea Palling and I would watch in awe as he launched a huge lead weight with a paternoster rig beyond the crashing waves with the help of another one of his homemade rods. Baited with either lug or ragworm, we would then sit on the beach and wait for the bell on the end of the rod to jingle, indicating a fish had taken the bait!

Uncle always targeted the cod or flatfish but invariably he caught dogfish. I well remember my aunt complaining about these fish, as they were very difficult to skin and gut. Uncle Corks used to tell her that it wasn't like going to the fishmongers and buying the fish you want. With sea fishing, he explained to me, you took home what you caught (as long as it wasn't too small) and either ate it that night or kept it in the freezer until needed. Now, that is fresh fish.

It was at about this time that I suspect my father realised that I had found a new interest. Always wanting me out from "under their feet", anything that took me away from the house was to be encouraged by my parents. With this in mind, dad bought me my first tackle box.

In the late 1950s, early 1960s, everything that was ever bought or sold was heavy. Strong lightweight materials were not, as yet, widely available. So it was that my first ever fishing tackle box was an ex-MOD ammunition box made from wood, with metal corners and clips and a massive all metal handle. It weighed as much as a small car.

Admittedly, it did "double up" as a very substantial seat. It was dark green in colour and had stencilled lettering on it, which from memory described the contents of the box. From inside the box, dad had removed the intricately moulded trays designed to hold munitions safely whilst being transported. It did nothing to reduce the weight.

Looking back, it makes me laugh to think that I put a few quill floats, hooks, line, split shot and some bread, total weight of less than a pound into a box weighing ten times that! Dad had bought this item from one of the many Army Surplus shops that had sprung up after the war. This one was called "English's" and ironically, it was on the opposite side of the road from the bomb crater.

The bomb crater was our destination of choice. We had been told by someone that the pond was created when a German bomber had been on its way to bomb London when it was attacked by a Spitfire and had to release its deadly cargo. There were two small ponds in this particular field and I suppose the story could have been true and to us boys, it was far more exciting to be fishing in a "bomb crater" than any old pond!

Looking back, me and my mates must have been very good at guessing the time. We could fish all day but would always be back home in time for tea. All done without the aid of watches or mobile phones! We would peddle our way to the pond on bicycles that weighed a tonne and were invariably too big for us so we could "grow" into them!

(Everything was bought or made bigger, on the basis that you would grow into it. My mother was very good at knitting jumpers but mine always had long arms, more suited for an orangutan, than a small boy. My fingers would poke out the end of the sleeves like little chipolatas. Shoes were packed out with newspaper in the toes so an extra year of wear could be achieved.)

These bikes were, of course, second-hand. My bike was particularly heavy as I had to strap the small car onto it using a pannier frame set over the rear wheel. This made my bike "rear up" like a bucking bronco and the only way to control it was by sitting well forward on the saddle and transferring all my weight forward onto the front wheel to act as a counterweight. This technique came in very handy later on in life when I started Youth Hostelling.

On arrival at the pond, we would heave our bikes over the barbed wire fence and make our way to the edge of the water. Sometimes we would go prepared for a whole day's fishing…jam sandwiches, water and, if we were really lucky, some penny chews. There we would sit, Ray, Alan, Colin and me. Our only bait was bread. It was always bread. Worms were rarely used and maggots were unheard of by us at that time.

I have read many articles about using bread to catch fish. There's punched bread, bread paste, bread flake, floating crust and more. I have never read about the method we used. This involved hacking off a lump of bread from home and stuffing it in the back pocket of our trousers. We would stand and fish and reach into our pockets to re-bait when necessary. As the day progressed, the bread became dry, grey and covered in fluff. Still, the fish would bite. It must have been very tasty bread, that's all I can think.

Despite the passing of many, many years, I do recall that we were quite successful young fishermen. We would catch crucian carp, gudgeon, rudd and roach. All from our little pond. I do wonder if that delightful place still exists. I would like to think that it does, but am not tempted to drive 150 miles from my home in Norfolk in case I find a new housing estate standing on the spot!

On hot summer days, we would sit around the pond and chat and fish and laugh. We would watch dragonflies snatching their prey on the wing and chasing off intruders from their territory. Damselflies and demoiselles darted around the vegetation surrounding the pond. Water skaters made intricate patterns across the surface of the pond, as did tiny whirligig beetles.

Little did we realise that 60 years later, this same small group of friends would still be fishing together and chatting and laughing and watching insects flying around them. Such is the strength of friendship and a common interest.

I pause here for a while to reread the last paragraph. Those days in my youth, when I hadn't even sat for my 11+ examinations, were idyllic. I and my friends were not to know that.

None of the families were wealthy. Few houses had a TV and cars were such a rarity that we would spend time jotting down car registration numbers as they drove past the top of our cul-de-sac. Meals tended to be basic. Vegetables were grown at home and in allotments. A joint of meat lasted for several days. Bones were boiled to make stock for soup. It was not unusual to have a jam sandwich for tea.

Clothes either came from the jumble sale or were knitted or, in the case of families with same sex children, clothing was always handed down. Social media was unheard of. Neighbours chatted among themselves. Anyone who needed help was given it by friends in the street. Doors were always left unlocked, even if there was no-one at home. My mother would "nip to the shops" leaving the back door unlocked, as, invariably, I would be playing in the "bottom field" or due home from school and I was never to be trusted with a door key!

Is it possible to recreate this environment for young children to grow up in today? To play in grass meadows? To watch birds and insects flying around? Can we offer children an insight into all that Mother Nature has to offer? Is it possible, in today's consumer-driven world, to show our young people the simple joys of being outside and just playing, without the need for a computer game to prompt imagination?

Sadly, I think not. So, without knowing how the world would progress, my friends and I would walk across the fields, through the woods, playing in ditches and swinging from trees. And we fished.

We did not restrict ourselves to pond fishing though. Not far from our road, across a couple of fields, was the River Wid. Not a big river, but to us it was like the Amazon. We fished this little meandering river for all kinds of fish. My particular favourite was the bullhead or millers thumb.

This delightful fish lives in clear, fast running water and tends to hide under big rocks on the riverbed. I would wade into the water and gently lift these large stones and look for the telltale shape of a bullhead and either grab it by hand or with a net made from one of my mother's old stockings and yes, the handle of the net was a runner bean cane!

We were convinced that "red throats" as we called them, were a separate species of fish. They were, in fact, male sticklebacks, that were in mating "mode" and would develop a lovely deep red throat to attract females. We would catch them and put them in a jam jar to inspect more closely. They would be joined by other sticklebacks and another little inhabitant of clear fast water, the stone loach. All would be returned to their watery home after we had inspected and admired them.

The delightful Wid ran over a road called Wash Road. This was in the days before local councils piped small streams and rivers under roads. Me and my friends would often stand by the side of the road waiting for the occasional car to pass through the ford and watch the water splash up from the tyres.

On hot summer days, we would stand in the way of the water splashing up and get a cooling free shower in return! We would build dams across the river and after watching the water build-up to create a decent-sized pool, we would breach the dam and watch the water gush through the gap and speed off downstream. We would spend our days outside on all but really cold, wet days.

Even on such days, we would play in sheds or homemade "camps" in the woods. Very rarely would we be indoors, as there was very little to do. All the excitement was outdoors and generally near water. We all carried knives. Not small pocket knives but rather large "sheath knives" as they were called. The blades were a good 6" long with a fake horn handle. We carried them in a leather sheath which had a loop to attach to our "snake" belts.

Now, here's a strange thing. These knives were bought for us by our parents. No-one considered them offensive weapons. As young lads, we never even thought that they could be used in an offensive manner. We used them for "whittling" bits of wood, sharpening sticks to make into arrows (the bows being made from "bendy" branches and string) and playing our favourite game of "stretch".

This required standing either face to face with a mate (the more difficult version was standing back to back) about three feet apart and after tossing a coin to see who went first, you would throw your knife (holding the blade) so it spun through the air and stuck in the ground to the left or the right of your opponent's foot. He had to move his foot to where the knife stuck in the ground whilst keeping his other foot in place. You then took it in turns to "stretch" your opponent until you couldn't stretch anymore!

This game became more dangerous as you tried to gain extra inches on your turn whilst being almost unbalanced (we probably were unbalanced in the head!) So, a small group of under 11's wandering around with 6" knives and no-one batted an eyelid and no-one got stabbed and no-one thought of stabbing anyone. They certainly were different days! This game was often played on fishing trips when the fish weren't cooperating and we needed something to occupy our time.

Our road was a cul-de-sac called Sunray Avenue and was "unadopted" by the local authority and as such was not tarmacked. It was full of potholes, which the residents would fill in from time to time, each being unofficially "responsible" for the area outside their house in the middle of the road. It seemed to work, although in very severe winters when it had rained and then the puddles froze, the ice would make the potholes even bigger. This is a problem encountered by Local Councils and the Highways Agency to this day!

Me and my mates didn't mind these conditions though as we could make the longest slides ever down the road when the puddles froze. There was a natural gradient anyway, from the junction with the main road down to where our cul-de-sac ended. One winter, we made a continual slide from Ray's house down to Alan's. That won't mean much to you but it measured about 150 feet long of uninterrupted sliding!

There weren't many people that owned cars in Sunray. Most of the men cycled to work or caught public transport. As a result, our lovely lumpy bumpy road remained like that for years. It was a road that I grew up to love, as it was where I met my lifelong friends and where all adventures began.

My parents had met and married during WW2. My father, in common with all young men at the outbreak of war, left his job and joined up. He was a bank clerk and was suddenly thrust into the army with its different set of rules and expectations. Dad was from London but joined the Royal Northumberland Fusiliers. I never knew why.

Meanwhile, my mother, who was born in Great Yarmouth, joined the WAAF (Women's Auxiliary Air Force). My mother was blessed with a good singing voice and would often sing with the "Big Bands" that toured the UK to entertain troops and "keep up morale". At one such event, at The Winter Gardens, Great Yarmouth, their paths crossed. Rumour has it that it was "love at first sight" and, after a whirlwind courtship, my parents married.

War over, my father re-joined the bank and my mother worked on the railways as a ticket collector. Many jobs, usually undertaken by men, had to be performed by women due to the terrible toll the war had taken on young men.

My elder sister, Stephanie, was born in 1948. My parents had been living with my grandparents, but decided they needed a place of their own and so it was that they moved to a small chalet bungalow in Hutton.

I arrived in 1951. Austerity was commonplace because, although the war had ended six years prior to my birth, some items were still in short supply. Much has been written about the excitement of seeing an orange in your stocking on Christmas Day or watching in awe as a car drove past!

I will not dwell on such matters as my memories do not look upon these times as anything other than happy and exciting. And so it was that my days were spent in the open and only inclement weather forced me and my friends indoors.

My sister and her friend Judith were "honorary" boys and allowed to join our gang, as was Alan's sister Jennifer (Jenny). Ray and Alan both had older brothers and they would occasionally join us on our tramps across the fields as would the girls, but, in the main, it would be Ray, Alan, Colin and me that hung about together, due, in the main to our common interest in fishing.

After taking my 11+ examinations, my parents dropped a bombshell. We were to move house. My father had been promoted to manager of a bank in Billericay and the family was to move to a flat above the bank. At the age of 11, I was to leave behind my friends, the river and the bomb crater.

However, in Billericay and just a short bike ride from our flat was Lake Meadows. This was a council-owned park and at its heart was a huge lake. To a young boy used to fishing in a pond and a small river, it looked like an inland sea! So, another chapter opened on my fishing experiences. A chapter that introduced me to larger fish and more sophisticated fishing.

# Chapter 2
# Billericay

Our move to Billericay coincided with a change of school. No longer would I be attending a small Church of England school in Hutton, but a huge "Technical and Grammar" school in Basildon New Town called Fryerns. What a shock to the system that was!

I had got used to the short walk from our house in Hutton to my junior school but now I had to catch a bus from Billericay to Basildon. To my horror, the school appeared huge and impersonal. There were almost 1,000 children attending the school compared with a few hundred at my previous school. At least I had fishing to look forward to at the weekends.

Lake Meadows Park is a short distance from the High Street and I would either walk or cycle there to fish the lake. Sadly, my Hutton friends rarely joined me on these jaunts and so I tended to fish on my own. However, many new school friends also lived in Billericay and I would often meet up with them when I was at the park. I think I was about 12 or 13 years of age when I realised that there was another gender!

Despite having an older sister, she was always seen as an "honorary male" because she was a bit of a "tomboy". So it was a surprise to me when I found myself attracted to members of the opposite sex. I would go to Lake Meadows armed with my trusty split cane rod with every intention of trying to catch some of the various species of fish lurking in the vast stretch of water.

However, increasingly my attention (see my previous comments on my attention span!) was diverted by girls from my school who would be attracted to Lake Meadows to sit on the swings or buy a drink from the cafe. It was **the** place to meet. My fishing suffered! I did have many successful days at Lake Meadows but looking back, I think I should have "upped my game" and concentrated on the large carp that inhabited the lake in those days.

Despite my experiences of fishing the pond in Hutton, I found it difficult to change my tactics to accommodate the larger expanse of water. I tended to float fish with maggots and as a result caught many silver fish, roach, rudd and even minnows. I also recall catching some quite decent perch from beneath the overhanging willow trees.

Sadly, during my time in Billericay, the local council decided that the old willow trees growing around the gravelled path of the lake needed to be removed, probably due to safety issues. These were the very trees that fish loved to lurk beneath whilst waiting for insects and grubs to fall from them. Without this cover, the fish tended to hug the islands in the middle of the lake, too far out for me to reach them.

Luckily for me, a school friend called Keith introduced me to the concept of ledgering. This was a revelation to me. I could put on a heavy lead weight (sadly actual lead was used in those days…deadly if consumed accidentally by swans etc) and chuck my bait out to the island margins. Mind you, that wasn't as easy as it sounds. I was still using a heavy wooden centre pin reel loaded with fairly thick line.

In order to reach the islands, I had to strip the line off and let it fall onto the ground. Then, with a mighty cast, I would propel the lead weight with the baited hook towards the middle of the lake.

However, the curled-up line would either refuse to unravel and get trapped in the eyes of the rod or, at the critical point of launching, the line would decide to hook itself around a stone or a twig. This wasn't too disastrous if the line was some way out, but if it happened early in the cast, the line would immediately whip back and a lump of lead and a fishing hook would catch your leg (if you were lucky) or your face (if you were unlucky)

It was whilst living in Billericay that my parents bought me a new drop handlebar bike. To my mind, this was a "proper" racing bike. It was certainly lighter than the heavy old lump of a bike that I had been used to. I also ditched the ammunition tackle box in favour of a canvas rucksack (ex-MOD of course).

This new lightweight mobility made it easier for me to cycle back to Hutton to see my old mates and fish the pond. However, after the bigger water at Lake Meadows and the bigger fish I was catching, the pond seemed too small and the lovely little Crucians were just that…little!

However, my mates and I decided we would cast our net a little wider and explore new places to fish. One of these places was the River Chelmer at Little Baddow. This involved a 25-mile round cycle ride.

Whenever I fished the Chelmer, it was a day-long trip involving loading the bike with fishing rods which were strapped along the crossbar, fishing gear was carried in my new canvas rucksack and food and drink supplies were put in my saddlebag. I would normally leave the flat in Billericay early in the morning as it took me a couple of hours to reach the river.

Normally, I was accompanied by friends but occasionally I would go alone. This was rather risky as the actual fishing spot was at Paper Mills Lock, which by its very definition consisted of extremely deep water and, at the time, I was a non-swimmer. It must also be remembered that there were no mobile phones in the mid-1960s and so when you went fishing for the day in the depths of the countryside, you couldn't call for help if anything happened.

But, as the saying goes, "ignorance is bliss" and as we were all in the same situation and didn't know any better, we just enjoyed being by the river fishing.

This was "proper" river fishing. Up to this point, my only experience of river fishing was the small River Wid and the Boxing Day fishing trip on the River Wensum in Norwich. The Chelmer is quite sluggish but had deep holes and gullies which held large chub, roach and perch. Some shallower stretches had a nice head of dace and there were gudgeon everywhere. My fishing tended to be of the "chuck it and see" variety. I wouldn't fish for any particular species because I had no idea how to isolate one type of fish to catch.

However, I do remember reading a book that suggested that roach liked feeding on silkweed. This is a slimy green weed that grows along the weirs and the sides of the locks. At Paper Mills, there were both. The weir prevented boats from travelling up and down the river, which is why the lock was built.

So there was I, a 13-year-old, non-swimmer, miles from home leaning over a weir and/or the lock gates to scoop up silkweed to put on my hook. Even as I write this I get shudders up my spine. What was I thinking?

Anyway, the silkweed idea never worked, as I couldn't figure out how to keep the stuff on my hook. I'd wrap it around my hook but it always fell off. I did persevere as my fishing book said I would catch a big roach when using it. Mind you, this was the same book that recommended using elderberries to catch fish and they never worked either!

As I became better at fishing, I realised I needed more sophisticated equipment, particularly a better reel. Fixed spool reels were fast becoming the reel of choice by coarse fishermen and on one birthday, I got my wish. My parents bought me an Intrepid fixed spool reel. This coupled with my split cane/greenheart rod made an impressive outfit. It was possible to use it for float fishing and ledgering. What more could a young boy want?

One of the joys of living on the High Street was the shops. Among my favourites were Woolworths and Ken Stubbs fishing tackle shop, which was located just off the High Street in Radford Way. Woolworths used to sell fishing tackle with the name "Winfield". This was the middle name of Woolworth's American founder, one Frank Winfield Woolworth.

I used to gaze longingly at the tackle on display but my pocket money never stretched enough for me to be able to buy any of it. I dare not ask my father for an increase and so it was that I started a car cleaning business. Living on the High Street, I was surrounded by businesses and one of them was an Estate Agent called Baistow Eves.

Luckily, my father knew one of the directors and so it was that I became the official car cleaner for all the cars on their fleet in the Billericay office. I also managed to find other customers and soon managed to save up enough money to buy several items of tackle. It must be said that the Winfield brand was "basic" but perfectly useable. I cannot recall ever buying tackle from Ken Norris during these years, but after leaving school and in receipt of a salary I did used to shop there.

I was now building my fishing tackle collection and, as all anglers will tell you, this becomes a lifelong affliction. I defy any fisherman to walk into a tackle shop and only purchase the item(s) they had intended to purchase.

Armed with some of my new fishing gear, I went on a boating holiday with my parents and sister. It was a holiday I shall never forget. I was nearly killed. The year was 1962.

My father had decided to hire a river cruiser from a company in Tewkesbury. This delightful market town in Gloucestershire stands at the confluence of the Rivers Severn and Avon. It was a mean feat just to get there. Cars in those days were most unreliable and roads were small and windy. Very few motorways existed, and so it was after a full day's driving we arrived at the boatyard to board our wooden cruiser. It was large and went by the wonderful name of "Silver Swallow" and, as my father discovered later in the holiday, it was very unpredictable in high winds.

I was in seventh heaven. When we weren't motoring along the Avon, I was fishing. I fished every time we moored up. I got up early to fish. I stayed up late to fish into dusk. I caught a beautiful striped perch, with their bright red pectoral, pelvic and anal fins. I had caught perch before, but these big river perch were heavier and plumper than I had ever seen. I was besotted with them.

Many years later, I read a book by Bernard Venables where he too waxed lyrical about the perch. In the UK, we are not blessed with as colourful wildlife as found in, say, the rainforests of the world. However, the perch would not be out of place in a tropical fish tank. I often see kingfishers when fishing and think, they too, would not look out of place in the Brazilian rainforest.

One evening, Dad had moored up at Nafford and after tea, I sat on top of the boat and started to fish. I noticed that on the opposite bank, there were some large willows drooping down into the water. These magnificent trees are beloved by fishermen as fish like to lurk in the dark waters beneath and hide in the roots that have pushed their way into the river.

Casting to the opposite bank was a challenge. I put on a huge cork-bodied float and lots of split shot but was still falling short of where I wanted to be. Dad asked what I was trying to do and when I explained to him, he nipped into the cabin and brought me a lump of cheddar cheese and told me to try putting it on the hook. I put on a huge lump of cheese, more as a way of getting across the river than anything else.

I held the rod high so the current couldn't drag the float back out into mid-river. It had just settled when the float shot under and the rod was nearly wrenched from my grasp. My heart was thumping. Something was trying to pull me into the river. I was sure of it. Dad was still with me and offered to take over, but I was adamant that I was going to land whatever it was.

The scrap lasted what seemed an age, but at last, the landing net slipped under a lovely fat chub. My first ever chub. It was only 3lb or so but to a young lad, I had caught a monster. That evening, sat on the top deck of our holiday cruiser, I caught several more chub from under the old willow. I went to bed overjoyed and excited about what the new day would bring. If I had known, I would have stayed in bed all day.

The wind had got up in the night and, as we set off upriver after breakfast, Dad struggled to keep the ungainly vessel on a straight course. It was decided that, due to the high winds and the fact that Dad had managed to drift into the bank countless times, we should moor up and wait for the wind to die down.

No sooner had we stopped than out came the fishing rod. My favourite spot was sitting at the back of the boat and casting near the bank. Dad had put up the wooden canopy and was below decks with mum and my sister. I had only been fishing for a few minutes when there was an almighty gust of wind. It ripped the wooden canopy off its hinges and, sail-like, it flew off the end of the boat, clipping the back of my head on its way.

The last thing I remember was wondering why I hadn't caught a fish. When I woke up, I was in the cabin with very worried parents looking at me and suffering from an almighty headache.

It appears that when the roof had flown away, it made such a noise that mum and dad rushed up from below only to find the canopy sinking into the Avon, mid-river and no sign of yours truly. It had hit me with such force that it knocked me out and I had slumped forward, nearly falling into the water. If I had, that would have been curtains. Dad found me and carried me down into the cabin and mum fussed over me until I "came to".

This was 1962. No mobile phones, miles from anywhere and no chances of getting to the hospital. So, as was the manner of things in those days, I was given a cold flannel to hold on the back of my head to ease the swelling and told to "rest". Dad was worried about losing part of the boat and mentally made a note of where we were so the boatyard could come and, hopefully, retrieve it later. Dad's description, I recall, was "It's near an open field with trees on the opposite bank". I doubt if the canopy was ever found!

After a while, I was able to get up and discovered, to my horror, that my rod was missing. Already upset by nearly getting killed, I was beside myself. We were still moored up and to placate me mum said she should dive into the river to find my rod.

She was a much better swimmer than Dad, having been brought up on the Norfolk coast and spending most of her childhood swimming in the cold, murky waters of the North Sea. Finding a rod in the River Avon should be easy. I'll give mum her due. She put on a swimming costume and dived straight in. It took several attempts for her to find it and I must say, both my sister and I were becoming agitated when she disappeared under the water for what seemed like an eternity.

Dad, meanwhile, directed operations, shouting words of encouragement such as "Over there…try over there" and "You've dived there before, go further out". But find it she did and order was restored. I think I was persuaded to abandon fishing for that day, as I had had enough excitement.

It was during this same holiday that I also got electrocuted in the rain after touching an electric fence. But that's another story!

# Chapter 3
# Still in Billericay

**Teenage Years**

However, I was now, at an age, 13 and a bit, when I yearned for more independence. Summer holidays had always been spent as a family. My older sister, three years my senior, had no desire to have her younger brother tagging along whilst she was sunbathing or chatting with new found friends. I well remember a holiday spent in Estartit in Spain. We flew from Southend airport in a "turboprop" aeroplane.

In other words, it had propellers! We landed in Perpignan, France and then drove by coach into Spain. It was an epic journey. The tour operator was Cosmos Tours. Our hotel was comfortable and the area was nice. My parents sunbathed all day and met and chatted with other holidaymakers in the bar in the evenings. My sister sunbathed during the day and acted very grown-up in the evenings. I was bored. I didn't enjoy sunbathing, I still couldn't swim and there was no-one my age to make friends with.

However, there was a small jetty near the beach and from this jetty, I could see fish swimming about in the clear water. That was enough for me. Every day I would take some bread from the hotel and sit on the jetty, feeding the fish. After a few days, dad bought me a cheap hand line on a winder from a local gift shop and my holiday was complete. I found a long bamboo pole and tied the line to it and wandered off to the jetty. There I sat day after day, catching colourful and very unusual fish from the jetty.

I took that pole everywhere with me. When I wasn't fishing with it, I used it as an oversized walking stick. I have a photograph of me, pole, mum and Steph. I am wearing long grey socks. I look a prat.

Following this first foreign holiday I decided that, although I loved my parents, I would prefer to holiday on my own in future and thus discovered the world of Youth Hostelling.

Luckily, Geoff, a new friend of mine from "big" school, also enjoyed cycling so we discovered the joys of Youth Hostelling together over the next few years. I never took my fishing gear with me as we struggled to get all our gear for a 3–4 week trip on the back of our bikes, anyway! The jam-packed rear panniers acted in much the same way as my overweight ammunition box tackle bag, in that whenever I leaned back on my bike, the front wheel would lift off the ground until I acted as a counterweight and slumped over the handlebars!

Still living in the flat above the bank in Billericay, my father decided to take up fishing as well, which came as a surprise to me. Dad decided to make his own rod but without the skills of Uncle Corks, he made one from an old WW2 tank aerial (bought from English's) with a glass fibre top section. The only problem was that he sanded too much off the glass fibre where it was to fit into the tank aerial (the ferrule) and, as a consequence it used to work loose after several casts.

This resulted in every six or seven casts the top section would fly out of the tank aerial and land in either the water or a tree or a bush. Dad could be heard cursing from miles away and if I was with him, it was very difficult to stifle a laugh. The worst thing was if he decided to join me and my mates, as it was so embarrassing to see my father with his rubbish homemade rod making a real plonker of himself.

Needless to say, my mates never bothered to stifle their laughter. They just laughed out loud until they almost cried. Looking back, it was a very funny sight. Local bank manager casts the top section of the homemade rod into an oak tree!

Having now found this new pastime, Dad decided to "up his game". One of his customers was a guy called Ted Brown. Ted was a proper coarse fisherman, much like Uncle Corks. Dad asked Ted for help and Ted was very generous with his advice. Ted was on the committee of The Billericay Angling Club (later to be The Billericay and District Angling Club) and Dad decided to join. I also joined the "junior" section, as did my good mate Ray.

We would hold meetings in a room above The Railway pub near Billericay station and before too long, my father had managed to get himself onto the committee. In fairness to him, my father did want to help the club in a practical way and thanks to his contacts in the bank, he located several waters that could be leased by the owners to the fishing club. One of these waters was Straits Mill in Braintree.

I remember visiting this lake with my parents and Ted to see if it would be any good for the club. It was a warm summer's day and as us, three guys set up our fishing rods, my mother, who was a very good swimmer in her youth, decided to strip down to her underwear and dive into the lake!

You should have seen Ted's face. Here was a dedicated fisherman who believed in stealth and quiet when fishing, being faced by my mother ploughing across the lake, kicking her legs and making an almighty disturbance in the water.

Despite all that, the club did decide to lease the lake and I believe club members are still fishing it to this day. Another stretch of water that dad found for the club was the River Pant at Shalford. When we visited this river for the first time, minus my mother, Ted, dad and I were walking across the field towards the river when Ted suddenly dropped to his knees. I thought he had either been shot or had a heart attack.

It turned out he had seen the river a few yards away and, in keeping with all good fishermen, decided to crawl to the water's edge so as to not disturb the fish. This was a new one to dad and me, who quite frankly, would have just strolled right up to the riverbank, thumped our seats down and probably scared all the fish away for the rest of the day. We had a great day there, catching chub, dace, roach and if I'm not mistaken, I think Ted caught a trout.

The fishing club grew in stature and members increased. They even used to hold an annual Dinner Dance at The Heybridge Moat House where cups and prizes from the various matches were handed out.

Ray and I used to join the older members on coach trips to various other locations. I remember fishing the River Rother in East Sussex and being amazed at how different rivers require completely different tactics. I suppose this planted in me a seed which was to develop over the years and see me fish for salmon in Loch Ness, sewin (sea trout) in South Wales and bass in Eire as well as many other species throughout the UK. But more of that later.

Of course, whilst all this was going on, I still had to attend school. This was not a pleasant experience for me. I was not academic. Dad was. He had a very successful schooling experience at Clarks College in Ilford, where he excelled at almost everything.

Even his sister, my Auntie Joan, was clever. She ended up being the second in command of Essex Education Authority and was a driving force of the Essex Youth Orchestra and spoke five languages fluently, including Russian! Dad was doing well in the bank and my sister was excelling at Brentwood High School for Girls.

Meanwhile, I was struggling at school. I lived for practical lessons, woodwork, metalwork and sports. I played football and rugby in the winter and athletics and cricket in the summer. I even volunteered for Drama just to get out of double physics or maths. When the school was looking for someone to play the Captain of the Capulet Guard in a production of Romeo and Juliet, my hand shot up. Even better was the fact that my good friend Geoff was the Captain of the Montague Guard and we had to have a fight on stage with real fencing foils!

For this, we had to miss quite a bit of schooling and have proper fencing lessons! Happy days. I must have missed dozens of physics, maths and technical drawing lessons. I quite enjoyed being on stage in front of an audience.

All this time, we were still living above the bank on Billericay High Street. Me and Geoff would go and watch Saturday matinee shows at the local "flea pit" cinema. Sundays would find me fishing at Lake Meadows or cycling back to Hutton or cycling the greater distance to the River Chelmer at Paper Mills Lock.

I lived for the weekends, half-term holidays and, of course, summer holidays. There was a period when Geoff and I spent several annual summer holidays cycling around the Home Counties, the South West and even Wales.

Geoff and I would book up the first couple of nights at a Youth Hostel in advance and then, having got a fair distance from Billericay, decide what direction to go in and take pot luck about getting into a Youth Hostel. Mostly we were lucky but I do remember on one occasion we tried to get into a hostel to the west of Romney Marsh but it was full and we had to cycle across the flatness of the marsh in a fierce wind to get to the Dover hostel in time for the night. We were 14 years of age!

I didn't abandon fishing but it did take a bit of a back seat for a while. I was still going on outings with the fishing club, accompanied by Ray and sometimes my father. I also started to fish a little pond that the club had acquired which was in Goatsmoor Lane in Billericay. It was a classic carp water. Lovely deep areas and big patches of water lilies. Looking back, it's such a shame that I had absolutely no idea how to fish it properly. Fishing was still a mixture of adventure, getting outside and messing around. Those that know me may ask, "What's changed?"

I vaguely remember another pond, dark and mysterious where I used to fish. It wasn't owned by the fishing club and it certainly wasn't a day ticket water. I forget its exact location apart from the fact that it was just outside Billericay towards Little Burstead. To reach it I had to cycle down Laindon Common Road, past The Dukes Head pub and, as I recall, on a bend in the road was a Public Footpath fingerpost. I would heave my bike over the stile and after half a mile or so, the path would emerge onto a field edge.

A little way further on the pond could be seen through a thick belt of trees. Thinking back, it must have been privately owned. This kind of detail never bothered me. I just assumed that any body of water, river, pond or lake could just be fished. I have to state, though, that this pond was not my favourite fishing spot. It was definitely creepy. There had never been any attempt by the owner to clear the trees or cut back the undergrowth.

As a result, I had to fight my way to the water's edge, getting scratched and cut by brambles and stung by nettles. However, it was well worth it. The water was dark, due in part to leaf litter falling into it over many years and also because almost all the sunlight was blocked out due to the canopy of trees.

In this unlikely watery haven, lived giants. Huge carp patrolled the surface, their backs breaking the film on the surface, like something out of the film Jaws. Looking back, I suspect the poor things were gulping down oxygen rather than seeking food, but all I knew at the time was that I wanted to catch one.

I tried many different methods. Ledgered baits would just sink into the silt whilst float tactics didn't seem to work either. It was during my trips to this pond that I discovered the joys of surface fishing. I would put a lump of bread crust on my hook and, about three feet up the line, attach a heavy float.

This would give me the weight needed to get the bait out into the centre of the pond where the carp tended to patrol. Casting was difficult. Due to the trees crowding in, an overhead cast was impossible. I developed a sideways flicking type of cast to overcome this problem, but if done too violently, the bread would fall off and the whole process would have to start again.

It was worth persevering, however, as the rewards were carp nudging double figures. Mainly common and mirror carp, they were in the 5lb to 8lb range. But they would fight like mad. My split cane rod would bend over so much it was a wonder it never broke. I rarely caught more than one fish each trip as the commotion of landing these carp was so great that the others would swim down to the depths and not move.

As with the bomb crater in Hutton, I often wonder what became of that dark pool and those lovely carp. I will not try to seek it out though, as I want my memories to be left intact and not be tainted by what it may have become.

As a young boy growing up in Hutton, I had become aware of the natural world surrounding me. Subconsciously, I had begun to absorb the wonders of Mother Nature. In fairness, it wasn't just me, but all the lads in our little gang were aware of and could identify birds, butterflies, moths and all manner of creepy crawlies. I suspect it started as we tried to identify fish and then we would find bird nests and identify the eggs and so on.

My parents had several books on nature and I would often refer to them to get the name of some creature I had spotted. Due to my inability to concentrate for too long, I developed a habit of looking around me whenever I'm fishing. If a fish was playing with my bait and the float was knocking from side to side about to shoot under the water and a cuckoo, say, flew across in front of me, my eyes would naturally gravitate towards the cuckoo and the bite would be missed.

This habit has stayed with me all my life. I don't regret it at all. I have seen some wonderful sights that I would otherwise have missed if I had spent all my time staring cross-eyed at my float.

My father was aware of my continuing interest in fishing and nature and wished to support me in these interests. Sometimes this would result in him suggesting we fished together. Dad was, like many of his generation, "old school". I cannot recall ever getting a cuddle from him when I was small. If I did well at school, which was rare, I would get a handshake or a slap on the back, with the words "Well done, boy".

I well remember a trip to the Chelmer with Dad. It was an autumn day. We had decided to try for chub. It was nice to be driven to the river rather than cycle there. Dad set up his homemade ill-fitting rod and I used my handmade greenheart rod. The section of river we fished that day was delightful. On the opposite bank was a small copse giving cover for any chub lurking there. I decided to fish with a lump of cheese using two large swan shot to help me reach under the overhanging boughs. Dad float-fished mid-stream.

Neither of us sat down. We stood fishing like this for a while. Whilst I cannot remember what we caught, I can remember, very clearly, an incident regarding a shotgun. There had been some shooting taking place in the distance, which was very common in those days. I'm not sure what they were shooting, pheasant maybe. Then, quite unexpectedly there was a massive "bang". Dad immediately dropped to the ground in a crouching position, covering his head with his hands.

On his way down, he thrust his rod into my hand. There I stood, a fishing rod in each hand, Dad crouching on the ground whilst shotgun pellets peppered the water in front of me. It all happened so quickly. Dad had reacted very quickly to the sound of gunfire and knew that it was nearby, in the woods on the opposite bank, in fact. But at no time did he yell a warning at me! This was something that, when re-telling the tale to my mother later, he got into hot water about.

'Didn't you warn Paul?' asked my mother.

'I can't remember,' offered Dad as a reply.

I know he didn't, otherwise why would I stand up holding two fishing rods whilst being showered in pellets?

# Chapter 4
# Stock Village

Dad was doing quite well in the bank. He was an old-fashioned bank manager along the lines of Captain Mainwaring in Dad's Army. You rarely encountered a bank manager under 40 years of age and my father was in his early forties when he got his promotion. He loved everything about the job.

Being very gregarious in nature dad got on with everyone. He was on several committees (including the fishing club) and loved organising things. He started the Billericay Cavaliers Luncheon Club. He told me it was "to promote local businesses".

I later found out it was more about a group of business people escaping from their offices for a monthly slap-up lunch at The Heybridge Country Club. I think they call it networking these days. Back then, it was meeting up with your mates and helping them out if you could.

We had outgrown the flat above the bank. Or rather, the bank had expanded and needed the flat for extra office space. We had to move again. Mum and dad looked all over the place for another house. I'm not sure if my schooling or my sisters' needs were considered, but in the end, dad decided to buy a parcel of land in Stock village, a few miles from Billericay and have a house built.

Stock is located on the B1007 between Billericay and Chelmsford. It has always been a desirable place to live and my father did well to find the land overlooking the "Green Belt" (land that could not be built on) and get planning permission for a detached four-bedroomed property.

Thus, it was that we moved to "Farthings" just as I had left school in the summer of 1967. Dad chose the name as it was all the money he had left after paying for it!

The move coincided with me joining the world of commerce. I was 16 years of age. I never had any idea what I wanted to do after leaving full-time education. Some of my school friends had definite ideas of what their future would hold. I think my parents had given up on me. I was perfectly happy messing around outside with my mates, either fishing, cycling or hanging around in the park. The world of work seemed light years away. It wasn't that I was work-shy.

In fact, whilst living in Billericay, I had started my small car cleaning business and earned quite well from it. I also did some part-time work at a factory on the Radford Way Industrial Estate. That was an experience. It was a packaging factory and my first job was to make up cardboard boxes from "flatpack".

I started with gusto, making up all the boxes given to me in about an hour. There was no room for me to move in the packaging area so I sought out the supervisor, who took one look at the completed boxes and gave me an almighty ticking off!

Apparently, the job had been "timed" as a half-day job and I had done it in a quarter of the time! He was not happy.

My punishment was that I had to sit behind all the boxes I had made up and not to emerge until the lunch break!

They thought I would be better on the assembly line and so it was that I found myself sitting amongst a group of women packing antiseptic cream into tubes. The language was what my mother would call "unladylike". But it was hilarious. I heard words I had never heard before and jokes that I didn't always understand. I loved it. I think the women took a shine to me because I was polite and helpful. I had the mickey taken out of me as they considered me to be "posh", but I didn't mind at all.

In fact, I think the experience has helped me in later life. I developed a good sense of humour based on friendly sarcasm and observational jokes. All my friends have the same humour and this, as well as the fishing, has kept our friendships going for all these years.

So, having experienced work part-time, I was now to be let loose upon the world of full-time work. I had always said that I didn't want to work in London or work in a bank. The trouble was, without any worthwhile qualifications, who would want me?

Dad got me an interview for the bank. I had to go to the Head Office in Lothbury in the City. I got in, mainly due to dad already being in the bank and because the guy who interviewed me was keen to employ more potentially good footballers for the bank's football team. I could kick a ball pretty well in those days, so I was employed.

I received a letter saying I was to attend my first branch on 4th September 1967 at Stratford. My starting salary was £370.00 per annum, with an additional Inner London allowance of £150.00 per annum. When I read the letter out to my mother, she looked slightly concerned. 'Where will you live, dear?' she asked, adding, 'Maybe your father and I can find you digs somewhere in the town. You will like it there, I'm sure and being Shakespeare's hometown, there is always plenty going on.'

I realised her mistake. 'Not Stratford-upon-Avon, mum, I'm starting work at Stratford in the East End of London.' Two complete opposites you could never imagine!

# Chapter 5
# Work & Ilford Connection

"Proper" work came as a shock to me. The daily commute from Stock to E.15 was a nightmare. Bus from Stock to Billericay, overhead train to Liverpool Street, Underground train back to Stratford and then walk to the bank. I could catch the slower "all stops" overhead train from Billericay to Stratford but that meant getting up earlier and I was already leaving the house at 6.30am.

In life, you hear a lot about "fate" taking a hand. Well, fate certainly played a huge role in what happened after I had been in the bank for about a year. I had started as the office junior and really enjoyed the role.

The staff were great. The "banter" was terrific and all the jibes and mickey taking that I had experienced at the factory helped me combat the comments from other members of staff in the bank. The office junior was always "fair game" when it came to jokes, but I could not only take it in good humour but I could also give it back…with interest.

About a year after joining the bank, another office junior was employed. A young man called Dave. Our meeting was to change my life in a big way. Dave, it turned out, had lived a very similar life to me and my Sunray Avenue mates, but in a more suburban setting…Ilford. Like me, he had a tight-knit group of mates who had grown up together and whose interest also included fishing.

Dave and I became good friends. Through Dave, I met his long-term friends from school and started to travel to Ilford for weekends, to party, go to pubs and clubs and generally do what guys of that age did. It was now 1969. I had been at the bank a couple of years and Dave about a year. It was the year of *The Rolling Stones* concert in Hyde Park and Ray and I decided to attend. Dave mentioned that he and his mates were also thinking of going.

The concert was massive. It was fantastic. The Stones were brilliant. But more remarkable than any of that was that Dave and his mates, Pete, Laurie and Hoppy, actually bumped into us at Liverpool Street station on our way home. That was the first meeting of the Hutton lads and the Ilford lads and what was to become an enduring friendship and one that has lasted over 50 years. Our combined group fluctuated between about 12 guys at its height to a "hard core" of seven. The "glue" that keeps us seven together is humour and fishing.

Whilst myself and my Hutton friends had been honing our fishing skills in lakes and rivers surrounded by countryside, the Ilford lads had been fishing less glamourous waters in Dagenham and Barking! Having said that, they used to catch some very large carp and certainly had as much fishing knowledge as me and my mates.

It was logical then that the two groups of lads combined to enjoy fishing trips, an activity we enjoy together to this day. But I'm racing ahead.

During this period of my life, every hour was occupied. Obviously, there was work Monday to Friday, including every other Saturday morning (this was the time when banks opened on Saturday mornings.) I was also playing football for the bank most Saturday afternoons, which was always a rush to get from the East End to Norbury in South London if I was working the Saturday shift. I also played for a team in Ilford with the unlikely name of "The Ilford Panthers"!

Between football matches, I had to fit in training, clubbing, socialising in pubs, girlfriends and fishing. Something had to give. It was the football. As much as I loved the game, I was never brilliant at it. I had my moments, once scoring a memorable hat-trick against a strong GPO (General Post Office) side. I suppose I objected to the sacrifices I had to give to train and play for two football teams. So, aged about 20, I hung up my football boots. Now I can concentrate on fishing…or so I thought.

One thing I have learnt about fishing is that to be any good at it requires total commitment. It's also a pastime that requires time.

In other words, it's not easy just to pop out and fish for an hour. If, say, your interest was reading, then you can easily pick up a book and read a chapter or two and put it down again. With fishing, you have to organise your tackle, load it into the car, drive to the river or lake, unpack it, set up, start fishing…all of which can take an hour at least just to get a float in the water! What I did find was that nipping down to the local pub to meet up with mates (and girls) took less time AND you didn't have to go and buy maggots!

So, despite my best efforts, fishing took a bit of a back seat during this period. However, I had by now acquired some fairly good equipment and over the next few years, it was put to the test on many occasions.

Although I had moved away from Hutton, I still had strong connections with all my boyhood friends. One of them, Colin, was a year older than me and, having passed his driving test he bought a Ford Anglia 105E (it had an inward-sloping rear window!). We decided to use it to drive to Suffolk and fish the River Waveney on the 16th June the opening day of the coarse fishing season—the "Glorious 16th".

We drove to the river on the 15th and, having found a free fishing section, parked up in a nearby lane and slept in the Anglia until dawn. All these years later, I still remember it as the most uncomfortable night's sleep I have ever had!

The sun rose on a wonderful section of the Waveney. Not a large river but beautiful nevertheless, as it wound its way through a meadow to a large slow bend where we decided to set up our gear. I remember how the river looked at this point, but have no idea of its exact location. I think this is common amongst anglers. We can remember a bend, a willow tree, long deep runs but have no idea what village or town they are near.

Colin and I fished together, both casting to the middle of the river where our ledger weights landed in the water with a satisfying loud "plop" indicating deep water. It wasn't long before our rods were arching round. Chub. Lovely, fin perfect chub. They will grab at most baits and the lumps of cheese we had put on our hooks were too much for them to resist. As we continued to fish and with a change of baits, we caught perch, roach, dace and eels.

One of the great joys of river fishing is the sheer variety of fish you can catch. This was the 1960s and long before the advent of modern-day "commercial waters".

I have some sympathy for anglers today who have limited time to go fishing. Desperate to catch fish, these people flock to a lake that has been crammed with carp (normally F1 hybrids) that are constantly hungry. Having paid their fees, these anglers can then cast out and are almost guaranteed a fish and another and another, each one a mirror image of the previous one. Uniform in size, predictable fight.

River fishing is totally different. No guarantees of catching anything. An understanding of "watercraft" i.e. reading a river is useful, although not essential. The joy is the unpredictability of it all.

On this particular "Glorious 16th", Colin and I did really well. It was worth the uncomfortable sleep in the car. I took a photograph with my Brownie camera of a very happy-looking Colin and he took a picture of me. We look very happy and contented. The photos were taken over 50 years ago. It seemed like yesterday.

# Chapter 6
# The Influence of Gerry

Up to this point in my story, events have taken a logical and mainly a chronological line. Now dates and events become rather blurred.

I know that I have stopped playing football. Geoff and I have gone our separate ways and no longer went Youth Hostelling together (in retrospect I rather regret that) and I am still living with my parents in Stock village. My sister married in September 1968. I was now in a steady relationship with a girl who would become my first wife (yes, wife number one…there were more to follow!)

This young lady worked for her sister. Her sister was a very switched-on business lady. She owned her own company and had an influential "sleeping partner" who helped her grow the company. Through my, then, girlfriend I got to know this person quite well. He was a brash, loud, self-opinionated, highly articulate, very intelligent man. He also fished. His name was Gerry.

Due to his habit of criticising almost everything, Gerry had few friends. Those friends he did have "tolerated" him more than anything else. He was wealthy, which helped, even if you are brash. However, I liked him. He was that rare commodity these days. A true character.

Also a complex character. I saw both sides of Gerry. He could be extremely generous and very kind. But sometimes, he could be brusque, even downright rude. But it was Gerry who introduced me to fly fishing. More of that later.

He once told me that in business you had to demonstrate confidence in front of customers and be forceful in your beliefs and the benefits of them dealing with you and your company. Outside of this working environment, you could be yourself. I know that in later life there was a little bit of that rather over-confident young man in me. However, I don't believe that anyone should have a "work-self" and a "normal-self". I think we should all just be "ourselves".

Anyway, I digress. My first fishing trip with Gerry cemented a relationship that sadly ended when my first wife (still my girlfriend at this stage) left me to go and live in Spain! But between these two events, Gerry and I had some great fishing adventures, as I will now describe.

Due to his wealth, he could indulge in his greatest passion…fishing. He had a boat moored at Burnham on Crouch for sea fishing. He had a cottage on the banks of the River Cothi in Wales used for sewin (sea trout) and salmon fishing and he had land in Eire where we would go for salmon fishing (and drinking). I was fortunate enough to visit all these places many times with him and enjoy the many highs, but sometimes the lows, of fishing with such a strong character.

His boat was a "classic" offshore wooden boat, more used to gliding through the water under sail. Gerry disliked anything that was slow and ponderous. He enjoyed speed. He instructed a local boatyard to fit 2 x 50hp outboard engines to the boat. They thought he had become confused and either meant one 50hp or 2 x 25hp engines.

They decided to fit a single 50hp engine. He was livid when he went to collect the boat and demanded that they fit a second 50hp engine. The boatyard owner actually wrote to Gerry and said they would fit it but it should only be used as a backup in case the other failed as if both engines were used in tandem, they would literally shake the boat to pieces.

This story was told to me by Gerry, as we exited Burnham on Crouch marina just before he opened up BOTH engines on full throttle! I had persuaded my old mate Ray to come with us as I needed a bit of support from a friend in case sea fishing with Gerry turned out to be "difficult".

When we reached the place, we were to fish, Ray and I were instructed to go forward and release the anchor. Neither of us are sailors so we struggled to release the anchor chain which had to be released gently and then the "brake" applied when enough chain had been lowered.

Unfortunately, we just pulled the release lever and immediately the anchor chain rapidly started to disappear over the bow. Gerry heard the rattling and yelled out 'don't let all the chain out or we'll never get it back' just at the point when all the chain HAD disappeared over the side and a length of rope then appeared. I panicked and grabbed hold of the rope.

That was a very stupid thing to do. The rope burns I suffered took weeks to heal. Luckily, Ray was there and helped me hang onto the anchor. Gerry was not happy and we hadn't even started to fish.

After getting the boat safely anchored just off the power station at Bradwell, Gerry decided he needed a "fry up" and wanted me to do it. Now I'm not a brilliant sailor. I'm OK if I can be above decks and able to see the horizon, but frying bacon, sausages and eggs in a small cramped galley on an old wooden boat pitching about in the North Sea made me feel rather queasy, to say the least. I managed to make Gerry his fry up without throwing up but never again will I cook on a boat at sea!

The fishing soon cheered me up as we caught a variety of fish, including flatfish, pollock, codling, etc.

My fishing trips with Gerry were always eventful. We made many trips to his cottage in Wales, which was situated on the banks of the River Cothi. This beautiful river has trout and sewin (sea trout) in it with the occasional salmon passing through. When I fished it, I would use worm and bump it along the bottom, tweaking the line with my finger to make the worm jump about enticingly. It's well known that sea trout are best fished for at night and so it was that Gerry and I would visit the local pub for dinner and a few pints.

In Gerry's case, it would be more than a few! I was always the driver, which I didn't mind. I'm not a good passenger and his driving was, shall we say, erratic! It also excused me from trying to keep up with his alcohol consumption. I always used to remind him that I couldn't drink as I was driving. That seemed to spur him on to drink my share as well!

His cottage was called "Clwtau" and enjoyed a fantastic position in a wooded section on the banks of the Cothi. We had a fair amount of success in catching our target species. Not only would we manage to catch sea trout but also many smaller but beautifully marked brown trout. Gerry and I wouldn't limit our fishing to the boundaries of his cottage but would travel farther afield and try other sections of the Cothi and Towy.

Looking back, I'm not entirely sure how we found these other beats on the rivers. I assume some research was done and permissions sought and permits bought, but knowing Gerry, he was just as likely to pitch up to a likely-looking spot on a river and start fishing. If he was challenged, he would either plead ignorance or press wads of notes into the bailiffs/land owner's hands and persuade them to let us carry on fishing.

I do clearly remember one incident when we were driving through the Towy Valley near Carmarthen and we saw a wonderful bend in the river. A farmer was driving a tractor alongside the river. I was instructed to pull over and Gerry jumped out of the car and walked towards the tractor waving his arms. The farmer stopped and I saw the two of them deep in conversation.

A few minutes later, Gerry was back in the car. 'Right,' he said, 'get the gear out, we're fishing here.'

I asked whether the farmer had given us permission 'Sort of,' was all Gerry said.

We did very well. We caught three sea trout and numerous trout. The beat was teeming with fish and all taken on the fly, which was fantastic. We were surrounded by hills and open countryside. It was a day to remember and all done on the spur of the moment. It was only a few days later that Gerry confessed that the tractor driver was not the farmer, nor was he the riparian owner of that section of river!

He was, in fact, a farm worker who told Gerry that we wouldn't be disturbed by the river all day provided we paid him a "fee" for turning a "blind eye" to our fishing exploits. Such things never worried Gerry but he knew I would feel uncomfortable about fishing a private section of river without authority, which is why I wasn't told the whole truth. Mind you, it was a brilliant day!

However, it was County Kerry in South West Ireland, where we had our most memorable adventures. Due to the vast amount of fishing gear we always needed, the only way to travel to Ireland was by car and ferry. Our favoured route was Fishguard to Rosslare.

Now, I've mentioned before that I'm not a great sailor and the crossing between these ports is renowned for rather "choppy" waters. The crossing time is about four hours, which doesn't sound too bad, but even four hours seems like 24 hours when combined with the choppy waters of the Irish Sea. Add to this mix a fishing partner intent on getting into the Irish lifestyle by consuming pints of the black stuff on the ferry before actually reaching Ireland!

I confess to being rather envious of Gerry's ability to eat and drink whatever he fancied without any ill effects. I felt queasy just sitting with him on the ferry whilst he drank his Guinness. Every trip was the same, I would drink coffee and look out at the horizon (on daytime crossings) and he would drink Guinness and chat to all and sundry.

Upon reaching Rosslare, I would drive across Ireland to our bungalow overlooking Rossbeigh beach just outside the delightful village of Glenbeigh. This was the 1970s and rural Ireland was in a bit of a time warp. It was like England, just pre-WW2. The pace of life was slow. It was always a mystery to me why Gerry enjoyed this environment, as he normally did everything at a million miles an hour.

These trips could last anything from a few days to a week or so. We always rented a cottage but apart from breakfast, we would eat out. Our evening meals were mostly taken at The Towers Hotel in Glenbeigh, at the time owned by a man called Evans. We would have our meals in the restaurant and then retire to the public bar where Gerry would partake in his favourite pastimes of drinking and winding up the locals.

It is said that you should never discuss politics or religion. Well, I would add that you should NEVER discuss politics or religion when tipsy and in an Irish bar!

I well remember one evening when we had been enjoying a particularly "liquid" session in The Towers and Gerry had been talking rather too enthusiastically about his views on the Catholic religion and the turmoil in Northern Ireland. The discussion was becoming rather heated and some locals didn't take too kindly to his outspoken views. I was sitting away from all this when I was approached by a guy who sometimes acted as our ghillie. 'Get him out of here, Paul, before it all kicks off,' he said.

I bundled Gerry into the car and drove the short distance back to our cottage. He was so drunk he collapsed on the kitchen floor and, being quite a "stout" man, I couldn't shift him. I decided to make him comfortable by putting a blanket over him and a pillow under his head and leaving him to sleep it off.

I was woken quite early by whistling coming from the kitchen. I dragged myself out of bed, my head still hurting from the drink the night before and wandered into the kitchen. There was Gerry, still in the same clothes as he was wearing the night before, standing over the cooker, preparing a full-blown fry-up. Sausages, bacon, egg, tomatoes, beans and toast. Never before had I admired his cast iron constitution as much as then!

Two hours later, we were fishing at Lake Caragh. This magnificent water held sea trout and salmon as well as some "wildies". We would either fish from the shore or hire a rowing boat from a local farmer. Owen, our ghillie and saviour from The Towers bar, knew all the best places to fish and most days we were successful.

I preferred to spin for our quarry and the lure of choice was Devon Minnows. They came in a variety of colours and materials. Wooden or metal bodies and various weights. It was all down to experimentation but once the correct pattern was found, catching fish was relatively easy.

As people got to know us in the locality, we became more accepted and Gerry's outspoken views were either ignored or disregarded. In response to this absence of a reaction, he stopped his rhetoric and actually managed to have "normal" conversations. However, it was one of these innocent conversations that nearly ended up with us having a criminal record for poaching!

Gerry had been talking to some guys in the pub about salmon fishing in the region and they told him they fish with nets in the bay. There was a narrowing in the estuary where the incoming salmon would gather before making their way upstream to their spawning grounds. We were invited to join them one night in their boats to help them with the nets.

We met the fishermen in a secluded spot and made our way out into the bay to cast the nets. I had never fished this way before and was quite excited to see what we would catch. It was a lovely night. The moon shone on the water as we cast our nets but despite several attempts, we caught nothing. It was decided that we have one last attempt before the tide turned and it was a good decision. We caught three salmon, the biggest of which was about 20lbs, a fine fish.

It was only after we reached the shore that it suddenly dawned on me that Gerry and I had, unwittingly, been fishing with the local poachers.

In his usual unflappable manner, Gerry just laughed at me and said 'What did you think we were doing, fishing at night with nets?'

It was an experience I don't ever want to repeat, particularly as I am totally against poaching. It did teach me an important "Life Lesson" and that is: never accept an invitation to fish, at night, with people you don't know! This area of South West Ireland is stunning. The coastline has wide sweeping sandy bays. Our cottage overlooked Rossbeigh Strand. The joy of using this as a base was that we used to get up in the morning, look at the weather system rolling in from the Atlantic and decide what kind of fishing to do that day. We could either go bass fishing in the surf, fly-fishing on the little river Behy or spinning on the Caragh system.

I enjoyed all locations and types of fishing. The bass fishing was only really safe to do when the waves were calm. Being on the West Coast the Atlantic rollers could be very rough, but if the conditions were right, there was nothing better than standing in the surf and spinning for bass. Having said that, I don't think I was ever very successful at bass fishing. Those fish that I did catch were more by luck than skill.

As mentioned earlier, I am a bit of a dreamer and am easily distracted. Spinning for bass takes concentration, but I could often be seen gazing at the inquisitive seals that would pop up in the waves to look at Gerry and me fishing. Overhead would be various sea birds, raptors and, as ever, rooks and crows. South West Ireland seems to have thousands of members of the crow family and my favourite in this group are jackdaws.

The wildlife here is stunning, as is the scenery. I have never forgotten a phrase that Gerry would often quote when we were fishing in a lovely location 'with a view like this catching a fish is a bonus.' How true now as then.

During these trips to Eire, I was always conscious of the political problems occurring in Northern Ireland. The only time we ever encountered any unprompted hostilities towards us was in Cork. We had caught a ferry from Swansea to Cork on this particular occasion to compare overall travelling times. It took less time to drive to Swansea as opposed to Pembroke, but the eight hours on the ferry were most uncomfortable.

Anyway, we arrived in Cork early in the evening and Gerry was desperate for a proper Guinness, so we called into the nearest bar. As we got out of our car with its distinctive UK number plates, we were sworn at and spat at, by a couple of locals. That was the one and only time we had any display of animosity toward us in all the visits we made to Eire.

As soon as we got chatting with local people and they understood that we were there just for the fishing, then the conversation would centre around fishing locations, baits, methods and, being Ireland, stories of "the one that got away"! Our previous "scrape" in The Towers Hotel was due to Gerry winding people up and, as such we only had ourselves to blame.

In the beautiful South West of Eire is a range of mountains called MacGillycuddy's Reeks. We would often fish nearby rivers and loughs. One day I noticed some smoke coming from a nearby hillside and asked Owen, our ghillie, if a fire had started. 'Not exactly,' he replied. 'It's someone making poitin.' (pronounced "potcheen".)

This illegally produced drink is very alcoholic. Some stills produce a drink that is 90% pure alcohol. Traditionally, the stills would be sited in the hills and only used when the wind could disperse the smoke. If the authorities did see the smoke, it would take them many hours to reach the illegal still, by which time the producer would be long gone, having been tipped off by locals. Owen asked Gerry and me if we would like to try some poitin later that day. I wasn't too sure but Gerry thought it would be great to drink 90% alcohol!

After a wonderful day's fishing, we drove back to our cottage and, after a wash and change of clothes, made our way to a local bar. After a very filling meal of lamb stew, we started drinking Guinness.

Later in the evening, Owen turned up and said he had something outside we may like to try. We wandered out to the car park and in his car he had a bottle of Whites lemonade, only the clear liquid inside was not lemonade. It was the illegal brew of poitin! Gerry took the first sip and uttered a few expletives. I was very nervous about drinking any but thought a small sip wouldn't do any harm.

Words cannot describe the sensation of that liquid going down my throat. Although the incident took place about 40 years ago, it is still strong in my memory. There was no smell and very little flavour but as the poitin went down my throat, it numbed the senses.

Firstly, my mouth went numb. It was like having an injection at the dentist prior to an extraction. When I touched my chin, I had no feeling in it at all. My throat went numb and, as it reached my chest, I felt as though a small fire had started under my shirt. Why on earth anyone would enjoy drinking this firewater is a mystery to me. Even Gerry, who had a cast iron constitution, couldn't manage any more than a few sips. I gave up after my initial sip and never again tried poitin.

It seemed to me that every trip to Eire had at least one memorable "event" that made it stand out. In most cases, these events tended to have very little to do with fishing, but it was the fishing that drew us to this delightful part of the world in the first place, so I guess there was a connection, however tenuous.

This next tale concerns land purchase and the rather unusual activities that ensued. Gerry and I had enjoyed a wonderful day fishing on the Caragh system (lochs and river) and, after a quick wash and brush up, headed to The Towers Hotel for a bite to eat and a few pints of the black stuff. Typically, Gerry had a few too many and after a few hours of banter in the public bar about fishing, talk turned to property prices.

Now, Gerry owned a few houses both in the UK and abroad and was always looking to buy more. He told me they were a solid investment as they will always, over time, be worth more than they cost.

Anyway, a man we hadn't seen before who was in our small group promptly announced that he had a couple of acres of land to sell overlooking the strand at Rossbeigh. Now I knew that the area was remote but stunningly beautiful. There were very few houses up on the headland, mainly due to the fact that the wind was, for most of the year, whipping in off the Atlantic Ocean and hitting the headland with all its might. It was not a place for the fainthearted to be building a house.

The talk turned from a casual "so how much do you want for this land" to "will you take such and such". I couldn't believe what I was hearing. It was about 11pm, in an Irish bar, half a dozen blokes all moderately drunk and discussing the selling and buying of land that hadn't even been looked at and, as far as I was aware, may not have been the guy's land **to** sell.

In vain, I tried to reason with Gerry. 'Look mate, you don't know the bloke, you've not seen the land, you don't know if it's his to sell and the location is windswept.' In typical Gerry style, my concerns were just waved away. He was intent on doing a deal for this piece of land and the seller was intent on selling it. At this point, I gave up and wandered off to chat with some locals at the other end of the bar. Half an hour later Gerry wobbled up to me and said, 'come on, Paul, we're off to see my land.'

It appears that a deal had been struck. A price had been agreed and hands firmly shook. Witnesses had sworn their allegiance to both buyer and seller...a deal had been done! Paperwork was a secondary consideration. Of course, the deal would have to be formalised by a solicitor but for now, Gerry owned a lump of County Kerry and he wanted to see it.

We all piled into the Citroën Prestige with me at the wheel and headed off into the hills overlooking Rossbeigh strand. There was driving rain, it was bitterly cold and it was dark...and everyone was drunk. Considering the seller was in the car with us, it took us quite some time to find the plot of land. The Citroen wasn't designed to go "off-road" but off-road we certainly were.

After driving up and down muddy tracks for what seemed like an eternity, we found the plot bordered by an ancient dry-stone wall. Most of it had fallen down and, typically in this part of Ireland, had not been repaired.

In the past, families would split their land amongst the sons and this tradition would go on for generation after generation. Over time, the plots got smaller and smaller. Some would be used to grow potatoes or hay would be grown to feed livestock. The walls were rarely designed to keep livestock in which is why their state of disrepair wasn't that critical.

This plot was large enough to have a nice house or bungalow built on it with stunning views over Rossbeigh strand. As we all stumbled about in the wind and rain, with just a bit of moonlight shining on us, someone mentioned that a pole should be erected to indicate that it had been sold and that a building was to be erected at some time in the near future.

Now at this point, I think tradition, drink and folklore got rather jumbled up. The locals were adamant that this "pole" should be erected immediately. Furthermore, it should, we were told, be the same height as the eaves of the building. So, we all scrambled around looking for lengths of wood that could be fixed together to form this huge pole. Someone had some baling twine and an old oil drum was also discovered.

The various lengths of wood were tied together, lumps of stone from the wall were tipped into the oil drum and the pole, now about 20 feet in length, was inserted into the oil drum and held firm by the stones. I took a photograph to prove the tradition had been adhered to and we all jumped back into the car and headed back to The Towers to celebrate the occasion.

True to his word, the seller met Gerry and me at a local solicitor the following day and the deal was made official. Gerry had his own bit of County Kerry. However, after completing the paperwork, it took Gerry and me ages to re-trace our steps from the previous night to find the land again. This time the sun was shining, the sea was calm in the bay and the surrounding fields looked green and very Irish. It was idyllic.

Of course, what brought us back to this part of Ireland time and time again was the fishing. We always had adventures when we were there, but the main aim was to catch fish. More importantly, to catch salmon. The wild Atlantic salmon (salmo salar) is an amazing animal. Their life cycle has been written about, had films made about it and discussed amongst anglers for hundreds, if not thousands, of years.

Our favourite haunt to fish for these magnificent creatures was the River Caragh. Spinning was the accepted method, although Gerry did have a go with a fly a few times but generally caught himself more than a fish. On one occasion, we needed to replenish our stock of spinners. We drove to the local tackle shop in Killorglin only to be told that the shop was closing down and all stock was being sold off at bargain prices.

Gerry was like a kid in a sweet shop. He bought rods, reels, lures, lines, hooks; in fact, I think he bought half the stock in the shop. Of course, he didn't actually need any of the tackle, but as it was cheap, he felt compelled to buy it. I satisfied myself with some Devon Minnows and a few Toby spinners.

When we, finally, got to the river, Owen, our ghillie, was waiting for us. We didn't always fish with Owen but he was born in the area and so it would have been foolish not to avail ourselves of his local knowledge. I was always fascinated by his fishing equipment.

Compared to the Hardy rods and reels used by Gerry and myself, Owen had a rod that looked like it had been broken into many pieces and stuck back together with gaffer tape. It was a big rod. I estimate about 12'–13' in length. It was made of glass fibre. The reel seat was crude, to say the least, the reel being taped onto the rod with lengths of black insulation tape. A few eyes were missing and those that were on the rod were of different designs. It weighed a ton. The line could have landed Moby Dick. It was a brute of a rod.

It was the only rod I ever saw Owen use and he would spin and worm with it. You will have guessed by now that his catch rate was easily double ours. I have watched him drop a spinner behind a massive rock halfway across the river, ease it around the rock into a pool and work it as if he had the lightest of carbon fibre rods in his hands. He could fish all day with this rod and never tire. I think I may have suffered from a bit of hero-worshipping about Owen!

The period was the early-mid 1970s. Fishing regulations were less strict than they are these days. Having said that, we never took fish that we didn't need. In fact, most of our fish were returned to the water.

However, we were partial to eating the brown trout that inhabited the small rivers and loughs in that part of Ireland. Fishing for these little beauties was great fun. All you needed was a small fly rod, a floating line with a sink tip and a small black fly. Some days, we got a take on almost every cast. It seemed the waters were alive with trout. We would take six or so and have them back at the cottage on a makeshift BBQ. Eating freshly caught and cooked trout with a few pints of Guinness whilst overlooking Rossbeigh Strand is my idea of heaven.

We didn't restrict ourselves to game fishing, either. I well recall standing on the rocks at Kells Bay and casting a lure into the sea to catch mackerel. It was whilst I was doing this one evening that I learned a very important lesson in sustainability from an old man fishing nearby. The mackerel shoal was within easy casting distance of the rocks and I was making the most of it. It was "one a chuck" fishing.

In other words, I was catching mackerel like there was no tomorrow. Then the old man arrived. He had a rather battered rod and an old wooden "starback" centre pin reel. He nodded a hello to me and cast out. Within a few minutes, he had two plump mackerel in his bag. He reeled in, picked up his bag and wandered over to me.

'Are you going?' I asked.

'Yes, I've caught tea for my wife and me. A nice mackerel each.' Then, looking at the pile of fish at my feet, he asked, 'How many are you feeding tonight?'

In an instant, I felt guilty. There was only Gerry and me at the bungalow and I had about a dozen dead mackerel on the ground. 'Oh, quite a few people actually,' I lied, then added, 'but I think I've got enough now.'

The old man nodded and wandered off. If ever there was an example of just take what you need, that was it. Mackerel are best eaten fresh. They don't keep very well unless you can cure them in some way. To this day, I hate waste and, in particular, food waste. I think I have a lot to thank that old man for.

# Chapter 7
# Friendships Grow

It's now 1973 and after six years in Domestic Banking, I decided to leave. An opportunity presented itself to join a Finance House which had been bought by the bank and so I was able to, in effect, have an internal transfer to another job. The big attraction was that this job came with a company car! As long as I could cram fishing gear into it, I was happy. I was in my early twenties.

It is around this time that events begin to merge into each other. I had a new job complete with a new two door yellow Ford Escort courtesy of my new employer, a steady girlfriend and a great social life. I was still living with my parents in Stock village.

Fishing would take place three or four times a month. Me and my mates would fish some disused gravel pits at Southminster during the Spring and Summer but during the winter we would often fish for pike at Abberton Reservoir in Essex. The Essex Water Company would sell tickets on a "first come first served" basis and numbers were strictly controlled.

This meant that whatever time you turned up, there was always room to fish. We used to fish off the dam wall by the roadside. The wall was concrete and the angle of the slope was quite alarming and near the water's edge it was always slippery. Great care had to be taken when landing fish. We went there specifically to fish for pike. I have always felt uncomfortable live baiting for pike. I have killed trout and sea fish in the past but always to eat and never just for the sake of it.

That is why I can't justify putting a live roach on a set of hooks to catch another fish, which I will be releasing, anyway. My friends all feel the same way. So, we would either use mackerel (purchased from the fishmongers) or we would spin. We used heavy Toby lures and cast them huge distances into the reservoir and we were remarkably successful. Most trips we caught lots of pike. A double-figure fish was a rarity but not impossible to catch. Most fish were in the 6–8lb range.

These trips started to become quite an event and took a different turn when John, one of our number, turned up in his works van with a full-sized gas-fired barbeque. This he would set up either on the pavement or on windy days inside his van. Yes, a gas-fired barbeque inside a vehicle within inches of a fuel tank. It's a wonder any of us are still here!

We would cook burgers and sausages. We had fried onions and cheese slices. We got through mountains of bread rolls. And beer. What started off as a few hours spinning for pike became a full-blown BBQ party. Other fishermen just stared in awe as they munched on their cheese and pickle sandwiches.

The Abberton Pike Fishing Trips became legendary and for many years were a fixture in our winter fishing calendar. Then one year someone suggested a Christmas pike fishing day on the River Chelmer. After the festivities of Christmas, it was lovely to get out in the bracing fresh air and spin for pike along the Chelmer near Danbury. This combined the thrill of perhaps catching a pike or maybe even a large perch whilst walking along the riverbank.

Even in the colder winter months, there are so many things to see. I have watched barn owls quartering frost-covered fields in their search for mice or voles whilst I've been fishing for pike. Inevitably, however, with so many guys chatting and laughing along the riverbank, most creatures decide to hide or fly away.

After several cold hours outside, a warm fire in a pub was always tempting and so it was that these sessions tended to end up with a few pints and crisps in a local hostelry. The river trips were never as successful as the Abberton trips but the afternoons spent in a cosy country pub more than made up for the lack of fish!

Fishing is split into three main "disciplines" namely Coarse, Game and Sea. Within those three broad headings are "sub-divisions".

For example, within coarse fishing are the carp specialists, the pole experts, those who prefer spinning or drop-shotting and many more different methods. I consider myself a Coarse Angler with a bit of game fishing thrown in for good measure. After my experience with Gerry in his small boat off the Essex coast, I never really got into sea fishing.

Abberton was the "go-to" reservoir for pike fishing but nearer to home was Hanningfield Reservoir. This huge body of water is over 400 hectares and over two miles wide. It is home to some huge fish, mainly trout, although there are pike, perch and other coarse fish in there. I was introduced to fly-fishing at Hanningfield by Gerry, who was a regular visitor to the place.

I didn't own any of the specialist equipment required for this type of fishing. Fly rods are lightweight pieces of kit, with a very thin tapered tip which allows the angler to, after a series of "false" casts, propel the fly out onto the water. Fly line comes in many weights and a variety of densities, depending on whether you want to fish on the surface or at various depths, depending on where the fish are feeding.

As with all types of fishing, manufacturers have convinced us anglers that we need as many varieties as possible. So, it's not unusual to find fly fishermen with reels holding floating lines, intermediate lines, sinking lines (fast & slow sink) of differing weights, colours and tapers (shooting head, sink tip, long head, etc.). The line has to be "matched" to the rod and so fly fishermen tend to have racks of rods in their sheds akin to a fishing tackle shop! Don't get me started about the various flies needed! Wet flies, dry flies, lures, etc., etc.

So, there I was, a fly-fishing "virgin" faced with this array of equipment needed. Gerry, though, was typically blunt. 'You don't need all that paraphernalia,' he said to me.

He gave me a Diawa glass fibre rod (rated #7–9) a Hardy reel ('just a bloody winch really…no idea why they're so expensive,' said Gerry), which was loaded with an intermediate line and a box containing a variety of flies. I was now ready to try my hand at fly-fishing.

Hanningfield has a concrete dam wall on which there are fishing platforms secured by chains. These allow for the platforms to be moved up or down depending on water levels. These platforms are also the safest place for an amateur fly fisher to try casting for the first time. Safety first is the main priority when a fishing hook is flying around in the air. For some of the time, it's also out of view being behind the person casting.

So, by standing on a platform with the vast expanse of the reservoir in front of me and a concrete wall behind me, it was considered safe for me to begin practising. I won't attempt to describe the intricacies of casting a fly line, mainly because I have never mastered it. All I will say is that it's frustrating, to say the least. Have you noticed that, in life, some people make some activities look easy?

The expert skier hurtling down a steep snowy mountain, a footballer weaving through defenders before scoring a goal in the top corner or a fly fisher casting a line far out onto the water in the teeth of a strong wind. Sadly, my casting is the equivalent of a skier falling over in the snow or a football player tripping over his own feet.

That's not to say I am completely hopeless, it's just that I struggle to cast very far and also have the fly line land straight with the tippet (the monofilament line to which the fly is attached) which allows the fly to land gently on the water. To see an expert cast a fly line is a joy. They can cast huge distances with great accuracy.

There are even competitions where competitors attempt to drop a fly in a series of rings on the ground that get smaller and smaller the further away they are. Rather like the expert skier and professional footballer, they make it look easy.

So, with enthusiastic encouragement from Gerry, I embarked on my fly-fishing hobby. I never had proper tuition, which in retrospect was a big mistake, but I did improve with practice. Some of Gerry's friends would be at Hanningfield and gave me hints and tips to help me to improve my casting technique. One of these guys was called Albert. He was a German.

At the beginning of WW2, he was captured after his bomber crashed during a raid over London. When Albert had recovered from his injuries, he was imprisoned but allowed out to work in the gardens at Hylands Park in Chelmsford. When the war ended, he was offered repatriation but Albert wasn't interested, opting instead to stay in England. He was a very good fly fisher and fly tyer. He was also more patient at tutoring me than Gerry. So, my casting improved and I even started to catch a few trout as well.

Some evenings I would drive the short distance to the reservoir and fish off the "natural bank". This was an area where, with the benefit of waders, I could wander out into the water, which shelved gently and then fish above the weed. Trout love feeding in weed beds for snails, freshwater shrimp, insect larvae and various invertebrates.

The weed beds were quite close to the water's edge, which suited a poor fly caster as myself. The midges were a nightmare buzzing around my head as I stood in the cold water but I had to remember that without them the trout would not be so numerous or so big. I used to try and imitate the midges by tying on a small black fly and even snipping off bits of it to make it smaller. Casting over the weed bed and drawing the fly back on a floating line, I used to have many successful sessions.

I would take the trout back to my girlfriend's house (she used to live with her sister near the reservoir) and gut the fish. This was another "skill" taught to me by Gerry and Albert. I have never been a "hunter" as such. The thought of shooting game birds or killing a rabbit has never appealed to me. I haven't killed a trout for years and these days I prefer "catch and release", but in the past, I have taken fish to eat.

It's rather hypocritical of some people to criticise the killing of trout but provided they are not endangered and the fish will be eaten, I don't see the difference between that and buying fish in a supermarket. The only difference being that freshly caught fish have a much better taste and quality of meat. No living creature should ever be killed just for the sake of killing it which is why I am so against "trophy hunting".

I remember my Hanningfield days with much affection. Not just because I learnt to fly fish there but because of the characters I met and fished with. The wildlife was also an attraction. Large flocks of duck and geese would gather on the water. Songbirds would feed along the water's edge, gorging on the flies and invertebrates. During the summer months, butterflies would take nectar from the bankside vegetation.

I am reminded of an unofficial "dress code" for fly fishers. This is a self-imposed infliction. I convinced myself that to be good at fly-fishing I had to **look** like I knew what I was doing. This meant wearing fly-fishing attire. As any good book will show you, through its photos and drawings, fly fishers wear corduroy or moleskin trousers, country check shirts, wellies and waxed jacket, preferably a Barbour.

So, it was that I invested in said attire. My girlfriend's sister bought me my first Barbour jacket as a Christmas present. This jacket lasted over 20 years and, despite my poor maintenance, it kept me warm and dry. I am of the firm belief that my "looking the part" philosophy enabled me to "blend in" with other anglers to such an extent that no-one saw my poor casting technique and tendencies to get into all kinds of tangles.

When, many years later at work, I found myself promoted into management, I followed the same thinking, i.e. dress as expected. Nice suits, shirts, ties and clean shiny shoes. Rather like my poor casting, my bosses assumed I knew what I was doing because of how I looked. If only they knew! I think the term is "winging it"!

# Chapter 8
# Mixing Business with Pleasure

I have been very fortunate in my life. Of course, like everyone, I've had my share of upset. Overall, however, life has been kind. Leaving the bank was a wise decision. I was thoroughly enjoying myself as Default Representative. The job involved me trying to get money from customers who chose not to pay. Various reasons were offered by these "defaulters". Losing their job, divorce, illness, dog eating wage packet, etc., etc.

My mentor was an old guy called Harold. All Harold wanted was an easy life, as retirement was beckoning. Days out with him were enlightening. I was annoyingly keen and enthusiastic and Harold just wanted to reach retirement without drama. Thus, it was that I would get the more "difficult" calls.

On one occasion, I had to deliver a writ to an address in a rather "dodgy" area. I was warned by my Office Manager that the borrower has been known to be threatening and aggressive. Undeterred, I drove to the address, early one evening (best time to catch people at home) and knocked at the door. Realising he may look out of the window, I parked my new shiny yellow Ford Escort round the corner and after knocking at the door, I stood to one side so he had to step out of his door.

What happened next is imprinted on my brain forever. I have always been a bit cocky. I'm not a big bloke but for some reason, I think I can get away with stuff on the basis that no-one would hurt me. When I played football, I would tackle like Norman Hunter. The problem with that is I was built more like Martin Peters! Anyway, the guy opened the door and, not seeing anybody, stepped out of his door. I then bounced into view and introduced myself, adding, 'I'm here to serve you with a writ.'

'Well,' says the guy, who I now see is huge and wearing a vest which seems to exaggerate the size of his arms, 'you can p#ss off.'

At that point, I should have done just that, but being a cocky little so-and-so, I carried on. Now, a writ is served if it just touches the person. I offered him the writ. He refused to take it, so I threw it at him and it struck his body and fell to the floor.

'I ain't picking it up, you little sh#t,' he said.

'You don't have to, it touched you, so it's served.'

Now the next bit was like a bad dream. For a big bloke, he moved very fast. I had anticipated a problem and had started to back away from him. He was like a greyhound out of a trap. I turned and ran. I vaulted the gate and, heart racing and headed towards my little car.

All I could hear from behind me was a lot of yelling, expletives and heavy footsteps.

I was going to die!

I fumbled for my car keys. Now, in those days, you couldn't unlock your car from a distance. Have you ever tried running, getting car keys out of a jacket pocket and then unlocking a car whilst shaking violently as a huge guy is bearing down on you?

I just managed to get in the Escort and lock the door just as the man mountain drew level with my side window. To say he was angry is a huge understatement. This man was incandescent with rage.

I think he was more annoyed that he had been outwitted by a skinny guy in a suit.

As I tried to get the keys in the ignition, he grabbed the little rain gutter that all cars had around the roof (I know it sounds odd but it's true). So, as I tried to line up the key he started to shake the car violently whilst shouting and cursing. The car was literally bouncing around as if it was going to come off its springs.

After what seemed like an age, I managed to start the engine and drove off with Mr Angry chasing me down the road.

I decided not to make any more calls that evening and drove straight home to Stock.

My mother looked at me and asked if I was alright. When I explained what had happened, she said to my father, 'Reg, you have to get Paul back in the bank. This Finance Company job is too dangerous.'

Dad ignored her. As usual.

I have to say, that my scrape with Mr Angry was not an isolated incident. I have been thrown downstairs, had dogs set on me, all manner of things have been thrown at me, but despite all that, I actually enjoyed the challenge and my perseverance paid off. I was promoted to the New Business Representative.

So, during this period, what was happening with my passion for fishing?

Well, there was a bit of a hiatus. I was in my early 20s. I had a steady girlfriend. I had a great social life. My girlfriend's sister had business interests in Spain and owned several properties out there as well. My girlfriend and I would sometimes be asked to "courier" paperwork out there, flying out on a Friday and returning on a Monday. We were having "long weekends" in Spain!

Friends would say 'what are you up to this weekend, Paul,' and I would say 'nipping over to Spain!'

Unreal, but true!

So, fishing? I did fish during this period whenever possible. In fact, me and my mates, who had adopted a group name of "The Bens" (a name that we still use to this day) decided to introduce a competition called The Liars Shield. This involved getting points depending, not on the weight of the fish, but based on the species caught. The rarer the fish, the more points you got.

Southminster pits were very popular as there was a great variety of fish in the waters.

Gerry had bought a lovely thatched cottage not far from Southminster, which was his mancave. He didn't live there. He used it as a "refuge" and he held some banging parties there. On one such occasion, he invited me and my mates there for an " Opening Fishing Season" party. It was held on the evening of 15th June because, at one minute after midnight, the day became The Glorious 16th, the start of the fishing season!

Me and the other Bens loaded our fishing gear and arrived at Gerry's cottage to have a quick drink before going to Southminster to start fishing after midnight.

The party was amazing. Gerry had invited Mercedes, a lovely Spanish lady who was involved in the Spanish side of the company. I knew her from my trips to Spain. To see my mates trying to chat her up was hilarious. A classic line from one of my friends that I shall never forget went like this:

'So Mercedes,' said one of the Bens, whilst trying to look cool and sophisticated, 'do you like Spanish food?' Her reply was lost in the laughter that erupted from the rest of us.

Shortly before midnight, we decided to go to the pit to fish. How we got there was a blur, but get there, we did. Overnight fishing in the 70s was nothing like it is these days. Modern anglers have technically superior equipment, including bivvies that keep out the rain and are well-insulated. Comfortable beds are also part of the package and some fishermen live the life of luxury when camped by the side of a lake for a few days. Not so our motley crew.

We had tubular framed camping chairs and green fishing umbrellas. By placing the umbrellas together, we made a makeshift roof and placed all the chairs together underneath. Unlike modern bivvies, there were no side panels to keep out the wind, so there we sat during the night, on our little camp chairs, wearing sheepskin coats and shivering like mad. It was only June, after all!

I can't even recall if we caught anything. I do know that most of us had a banging headache and decided that never again would we go all-night fishing immediately after a party.

Life continued to be good to me and my mates. We all had good jobs and money in our pockets. We had steady girlfriends. We spent our free time going to pubs and parties. At least a couple of times a month, we would fish.

Our fishing equipment became more sophisticated. Hollow glass rods were being mass-produced and Ray and I invested in the same make, an ABU 10' light ledger rod. This rod, coupled with an Intrepid fixed pool reel, became my all-rounder combo. I used it for light ledgering, spinning and even a bit of float fishing. I was still fishing with Gerry and took the rod to Wales and Eire. With it, I caught pike, bream, carp, barbel, sewin and even salmon. 45 years later, Ray still has his ABU but mine has gone, I know not where.

# Part 2

# Chapter 9
# Assorted Tales

As you go through life, the order in which things happen become muddled. I'm not talking about major events such as marriage, or, as in my case, marriage, divorce, marriage, divorce, marriage. No, I am talking about activities, which, at the time become part of everyday life.

It's only as I reach old(ish) age that I wish I had kept a diary. I am in awe of those people who keep a detailed diary, with every minute detail of the day's events being noted only to be regurgitated many years later to form a thick tome, which, within it's pages, recounts every activity from days many years previously.

So, at this juncture in my book, I have decided not even to attempt to get the dates in order. My angling adventures started to melt into one long yarn from the date of my first marriage, 1976 and punctuated by more detailed annual fishing trips in the pursuit of barbel. These annual trips have, at the time of writing, been undertaken, without a break for 42 years and counting. More of this later.

This section then relates to assorted tales, not date specific, but involving my love of fishing.

*The man who introduced me to fishing, Harold Cory "Uncle Corks" with his wife, Mary*

*The author, aged 9, at Sea Palling beach, Norfolk holding*
*2 x dogfish*

*Fishing the River Avon whilst my mother, on Silver Swallow, and my sister look on. Both appear bored*

*The morning after the night before. From L to R standing: Laurie (HB) and Paul (Baldy). Seated L to R, Andy (Boy) and Pete (Dad)*

*The ambulance that took us to Ringwood and into Ringwood Carnival*

*Lunch time away from the River Wye. L to R: Pete (Hoppy), John
(Molsky), Me (Baldy) Ian (Nice Bloke) Ray, Pete (Dad), Laurie (HB). Note
the guy in the background carrying his lump of woord. He always carried
wood about!*

*Hoppy, Baldy, Dad and Molsky with our beloved Trooper*

*The best fishing mates anyone could have. L to R: HB, Andy Boy, Al, Dad.
Front, Molsky and Ray*

*The author with a lovely Wye barbel*

## Rutland Water

Rutland Water is a huge reservoir in the county of Rutland. By surface area, it is the largest reservoir in England and one of the largest artificial lakes in Europe.

It was formed by flooding a valley in 1976 with water pumped in from the Rivers Nene and Welland. It's surface area is 10.86 square kilometres (4.19sq. miles) and holds 124 million cubic metres of water. It is very deep, about 100 feet at its deepest. All this is set in 3,100 acres of countryside and has a 23 mile perimeter track popular with cyclists and walkers.

It holds many attractions for anglers as well. The water is stocked with rainbow and brown trout. There are also healthy numbers of coarse fish, including pike, perch and zander. All my fishing there has been for the trout.

I had improved my fly-fishing thanks to Gerry, by regularly visiting Hanningfield reservoir. Hanningfield is a baby compared to Rutland, with a surface area of only 4.03 square kilometres. However, the basics are the same, surely? Not quite. Most of my fly-fishing at Hanningfield had been from the damn wall or the "natural bank" as it was known.

My friends and I made many trips to Rutland. Here are some of my recollections of just a few of the incidents that befell us.

### The missing anchor

Ray and I were sharing a boat during a particularly windy day. Rutland has real waves, whitecaps they're called when the wind gets up. We motored across the water to Old Hall

Bay, where, we had been told by the bailiff, the trout were feeding hungrily.

It took forever to get there. We decided to moor in a likely-looking area about 100 yards offshore. Ray grabbed the anchor and chucked it into the reservoir. The chain and then the rope snaked out into the water and kept going, until at last the end of the rope—disappeared over the side. It hadn't been tied on. We had lost the lot. Anchor, chain and anchor rope. Memories of the trip in Gerry's boat years before came flooding back. We had almost lost that anchor as well.

This time, we had done a proper job and lost the lot. We were on the far side of Rutland, as far away from the Fishing Lodge as possible. There was no way we could stay and fish without an anchor and we didn't have a drogue. There was nothing for it, we had to motor back and get another anchor.

Half an hour later, we were back at the pontoons. The bailiff was working outside the gutting shed. Ray and I drew straws to decide who should give him the bad news and ask for another anchor. Ray lost. As we approached him, we sensed he wasn't having the best of days.

The bailiff looked up and, just as I expected him to ask for the anchor, Ray started to giggle uncontrollably. It was one of those stifled laughs that the more you try to control, the more you laugh. And it's infectious. I started to laugh as well. The bailiff asked what was wrong. Between tears of laughter, Ray explained that we had chucked the anchor overboard and lost the lot.

The bailiff wasn't laughing. He demanded that we take him to the boat. When we got to the boat, he asked us to describe the anchor. He then lightened up. It appeared that the anchor we had lost was not owned by Anglia Water but was a privately owned anchor that someone had used as a supplementary anchor due to the high winds.

They had obviously forgotten to remove it when they left, which is why it was untied. The bailiff thought they would be back to retrieve it. I have no idea what he told them but it's not our fault the anchor was lost. Was it?

### The runaway boat

On another occasion, there were six of us fishing in three boats. The morning session had been fairly uneventful and we had decided to meet up in the Fishing Lodge cafe for lunch and a beer. After lunch, we went to the boats. Using an outboard engine is fairly straightforward.

Sometimes, however, when you're sitting in the stern of a boat with the tiller in your hand and a twist grip for the throttle but are facing forward, things can become disorientated. And so it was with Pete (Hoppy). Our first two boats were leaving the pontoons. There are strict instructions to keep the speed down in the area of the pontoons but as Hoppy untied his boat and opened up his throttle, he sensed he was going slightly too fast. What happened next can only be described as something out of a "Carry On" film.

Instead of reducing the throttle, he opened it up and started to power towards the bank about 50 yards away. Panicking, he tried to steer the boat away from dry land and, in so doing accelerated even more! We watched in disbelief.

The banking was approaching fast and in a matter of a few short seconds the boat left the water and powered up the bank, slicing through grass and gravel. The propeller was spinning away and cutting a nice groove in the earth. It was hilarious.

There was now a healthy crowd of onlookers watching these antics and, as the poor boat came to rest completely out of the water, a huge cheer went up. Ray and me who were sharing a boat, collapsed helplessly with laughter at the bottom of our boat. I couldn't move for five minutes due to the pain in my stomach from laughing.

**Sunburn and the beetle.**

On some of our trips to Rutland Water, we would stay overnight in a B&B to enjoy two days of fishing and an evening meal with a few pints in a local pub. On this particular long weekend, we stayed at a B&B called "Chestnuts". We would drive to the reservoir and fish it all day before booking into "Chestnuts".

It was a very hot day. The huge slab of water was still and calm. Again, there were six of us in three boats. We all decided to motor off to the middle of the reservoir and fish the deeper water, assuming the trout may like the deeper, cooler water. Although a couple of the lads knew a little about trout feeding habits, none of us was an expert. Nowhere near!

We all sat in our open boats, shirts off, getting a nice tan. The fishing was OK. Nothing memorable, although one of the guys was particularly successful in using a string of buzzers on a floating line. This was known as the "fishing line" technique.

I am not a very good fly fisherman and this idea appealed to me as after putting a goldhead fly on the tip, two or three "buzzers" were tied on by means of droppers to the main tippet length and after casting out, the line was tightened and all you have to do is hold the rod and "tweak" the line every now and then. The floating line would sit on the surface and the monofilament line (tippet) had the buzzers hanging down just under the surface. All you have to do is wait for the trout to swim past and grab the flies.

As the sun rose in the sky, we decided to don our T-shirts and caps. All except one. John had decided to get a tan to beat all tans. Despite our advice, he refused to cover up and, it has to be said he did resemble a big red lobster by the time we packed up for the day.

We drove back to "Chestnuts" and enjoyed a shower and a "spruce up". We had booked a table at a nearby pub which was within walking distance.

When we got to the entrance, I noticed what I thought were moths flying around the light outside the front door. One by one, we walked into the pub. The last person through the door was John. Now John has a moustache, but after hearing him shout out, we looked around to see that his moustache was moving. John was clawing at it and yelling, 'get it off, get it off.'

I walked over and saw that it was a cockchafer or "maybug" and its legs, which have little hooks on them, had got well and truly tangled in John's moustache. It was a funny sight. A big beetle, flapping its large wing cases, trying to extract itself from John's top lip and John yelling out 'Geroff, Geroff!'

Finally, the insect got away and went crashing into the lights in the pub. We left the landlord to deal with it!

But that was just the beginning of John's terrible evening. We all had a pint and perused the menu. Being animals of habit, we ordered steaks, we loved steak and we were all hungry. John had gone a bit quiet and we all thought that he was still getting over being attacked by a large insect.

Sadly, that was not the reason for him going quiet. Poor John had sunstroke. As the steaks arrived, John got up from the table and announced that he didn't feel too good and was going to walk back to the digs. Now we had a dilemma. Should one of us walk back with him to make sure he was OK and didn't flake out? But his steak and trimmings had just arrived and that got precedence.

As John walked out of the pub, we all stabbed at his plate with knives and forks to claim his steak and mushrooms and chips. It was very unseemly. But typical of us.

Later in the evening, as we were having yet another pint, somebody suggested that one of us should nip back to the B&B and check on John. No-one did.

### Loch Ness and the Monster

A dear friend (and lapsed fisherman) of mine married a lovely Scottish lass. Her brother helped their parents with the running their hotel in Scotland at a place called Spean Bridge and knowing about my love of fishing, I was invited there for a long weekend to fish the rivers and lochs. I didn't need to be asked twice.

The only drawback was that I was to go alone and it was a punishing drive, particularly as my company car at the time was a diesel Land Rover Discovery. Not the most nimble of vehicles for motorway driving. So it was that I found myself heading North on the M1 out of Watford with fly-fishing gear and clothes for all kinds of weather.

It's almost exactly 500 miles door to door and it took me a full day to do the drive, having started out early and getting there very late. However, as the hotel is in the depths of Scotland, the one thing you have to have (even after a long drive) as you arrive is a "wee dram". Let's just say that when I finally got to bed, I slept like a log.

The following day, I was taken out by Alistair (the son) to fish near the Caledonian Canal. It involved some sightseeing near Fort William and there were wonderful views of Ben Nevis. From memory, I think we fished Loch Oich which is one of the lochs linked up by the canal. The area is stunning and as with many fishing locations, I am always reminded of Gerry's phrase "catching a fish is a bonus".

My host was very attentive but he had a "day job" to do at the hotel and so it was that he arranged for me to fish one day with a local ghillie. We were to meet at Drumnadrochit on the banks of the famous Loch Ness. I was to fish for salmon and all the fishing gear would be provided.

I arrived at the appointed time, almost bursting with excitement. I parked at the exact location but all I could see was an old man puffing on a pipe with a large dog by his side. And a tired, worn out, knackered rowing boat bobbing about at the water's edge. You've guessed it, he was the ghillie and that was his boat. It didn't even have a cuddy and it looked like rain.

Pleasantries over with, we got in the boat, dog as well and headed out into the bay overlooked by Urquhart Castle. My misgivings were soon replaced by joy at being on such a famous stretch of water and fishing for salmon.

Now I wouldn't say I am the most fastidious angler when it comes to maintaining my fishing tackle, but I do clean and oil my reels and if a ring on a rod needs repairing, I repair it.

Likewise, my lures, fly line, flies etc are well looked after and maintained. Not so the tackle I was handed in the boat. The rod, a very stout 9' spinning rod, had no matching rings. They were different styles and although followed the accepted rule of the biggest ring near the butt end and an incremental decrease in ring size towards the tip, the jump in sizes was quite alarming.

Furthermore, they were held onto the rod by whipping of different colours, grades and strengths. Now, it can be argued that as long as a rod is functional, it doesn't have to be pretty, but this was one ugly, heavy rod. The reel was no better. It was a large fixed spool reel, filled to capacity with what was salt water monofilament line of, at a guess, 30lb breaking strain.

The last time the reel was oiled was when it left the factory about 20 years before I used it. The bale arm was rusty, as was the handle. The Toby lure was like nothing I had seen before. I think it had started out as trying to mimic a small silverfish, but now looked like it was trying to imitate a bit of wreckage salvaged from a sunken ship. The two sets of treble hooks would definitely have given me tetanus if I had pricked myself on them.

So, there I was with my "fishing tackle provided", chugging along the shores of the mighty Loch Ness with a pipe-smoking ghillie and large dog for company. The little Seagull engine was doing a sterling job, but it did occur to me that if the engine is as well maintained as the fishing gear, I think we could be in big trouble when it conks out!

'Go on then, lad,' said the ghillie, 'cast out and we'll troll for the salmon.'

I heaved the rod up and cast out the rust-encrusted lure, more in hope than confidence. And so we chugged on, me looking at the wonderful scenery, the ghillie puffing on his pipe and the hound looking mournfully at dry land. This continued for about an hour and then disaster.

'Stop,' I yelled. 'I've got snagged on a rock, I think.'

The engine was cut and I tried to free the lure...which then started to move, faster and faster. Line ripped off the reel at an alarming rate, the old dry clutch making a hell of a noise.

'You've got one. You've got one,' exclaimed the ghillie.

And I had. I had hooked a salmon. In Loch Ness. Near Urquhart Castle, where the monster lives. This was the stuff of dreams. Or a nightmare if I couldn't land it. Even the dog was looking excited by now.

The battle was made more difficult due to the state of the tackle. I swear I heard the rod crack at one point and I know the reel was creaking, but I stuck at the task and after what seemed like an eternity, we had a lovely 9lb grilse in the boat. Not the biggest salmon in the world but my first Scottish salmon and with a lovely silver body.

All three of us were excited (yes, I include the dog) but, as is the manner of these things, the salmon was "despatched" swiftly by the ghillie. In the 1990s, this was commonplace but feelings towards this, including my own, have changed. I would no longer take a fish for the table, preferring to release it back to its watery home to live out its natural life.

Despite my best endeavours with the unwieldy rod, I was unable to catch another salmon and so it was decided to try some brown trout fishing and I was about to receive the most unusual instructions from my new pipe-smoking friend. He manoeuvred the little boat alongside a small rocky cliff rising out of the edge of the loch and cut the engine.

'Now, lad, do as I tell you.' I was instructed.

Whereupon, I was told to cast my fly, a small drab black thing, so it struck the cliff face. I had taken my 91/2' Hardy rod with me and a box of my own flies and was very confident and competent at carrying out these orders. It did seem unusual, but as the first cast hit the rock face and the fly dropped into the water, I got an instant take! It took me by surprise and I was late for the strike.

On my second attempt, I managed to land a lovely little brown trout which I released. And so we gently drifted along the edge of Loch Ness with me casting against the rock and allowing the fly to fall into the water and getting takes almost one in three.

The theory, it was explained to me, is that the trout are waiting for insects to fall into the water that has been on the rock face. They have learnt that if they patrol this area where the water is very deep, food will be presented to them. Interestingly, if my cast was a foot or so short of hitting the rock, I didn't get a take.

This being Loch Ness and me being a chatty sort of a guy, I asked about the monster. The reply I got was astonishing. The conversation went something like this:

Me: 'So, have you ever seen the Loch Ness monster?'
Him: 'Och Aye.'
Me: (incredulously) 'What! You've actually seen it?'
Him: 'Aye. Four times.'

There followed a conversation that will live with me to the end of my life. I was told that on one occasion he was fishing, on his own, of course, in the bay overlooked by Urquhart Castle, when there was a swirl in the water. Thinking it was a salmon moving, he cast a lure towards it but instead of catching a salmon, he nearly hooked the monster. Its huge grey back, I was told, raised out of the water and the bow wave rocked the little boat as it was only about 40' away.

By this time, I was thinking either he's mad or he had one wee dram too many. The story continued and described the colour of the beast's skin and the scars upon it. He didn't see any more than the huge back, as it then sunk back into the depths. That was his closest encounter, the other three sightings were from a distance, two from the boat and once from the road that runs around Loch Ness.

What impressed me most of all was that the story wasn't dramatic as such. He didn't say that it had giant fangs or that it thrashed the water. It was a huge body that broke the surface and sunk again. In much the same way as a whale would act.

I believed him. I think he DID see something that day and possibly those other days as well. I have witnessed similar things myself. Only last year I was driving back from an evening fishing match in rural Norfolk and a large black, panther-like cat crossed the road ahead of me in full view of my very powerful headlights. There have been rumours of such a creature living around that area for years.

Had I seen it? I would swear that I had. Likewise, had the ghillie seen the Loch Ness monster? Yes, I think he had or rather he had seen "something".

My day on the loch was coming to an end but hadn't quite finished. After getting back to shore, I was invited back to the ghillies house for a quick tot of whisky to celebrate our wonderful day. I diligently followed his car along the road and then up a small lane and then, climbing more and more steeply, onto a rough track. There, at the top, was a lovely bungalow. I seem to recall it was timber clad.

We went into the lounge and I realised my new friend lived on his own. It was very much a "man's dwelling". Out came the whisky and I was given a huge amount. I am not a spirit drinker at all and as I was conscious of the drive back to the hotel, I asked for a mixer. Well, you would have thought I'd asked for a million pounds!

The look I got was unbelievable. I was told in no uncertain terms that I could have "a drop" of water. And a drop it was! Luckily for me, the dog needed feeding, so whilst that was being done, I poured most of my whisky into a pot plant.

We arranged to meet at the hotel later when I would buy my friend as much whisky as he wanted for giving me such a wonderful day on Loch Ness.

I arrived back at the hotel, gave the chef the salmon and went to my room for a shower and change of clothes.

After dinner (the salmon was lovely), I met up with Alastair and my new friend in the bar and as the evening grew on and the whisky flowed, my grilse became a full-blown Atlantic salmon of over 20lbs.

I haven't named this amazing man that made such wonderful memories for me, but I will now.

His name was Bill Davidson and he was ghillie for Killianan Game Fishing. Bill was a character. Although I only met him the once, I feel we are connected. I have always liked "characters" (hence my friendship with Gerry) and Bill was certainly a character. He also "looked the part". Tweed clothing, wellies, pipe, big moustache and a "lived in" face.

A view on everything and before the days of Political Correctness, he said what he wanted to say. A well-read man and an excellent angler, although lousy at maintaining his gear. It could be, though, that the tackle I was given was for Sasanachs! That wouldn't surprise me.

We stayed in touch by letter for a few years. I never returned, which is a huge regret of mine. Some years later, I received a lovely letter from Bill's son advising me that his father had died and whilst going through his things, he found several letters from me and thought I should know of his dad's passing.

So, thanks Bill for leaving me with happy memories of salmon, Loch Ness, the monster, whisky and lively conversation. R.I.P.

### Lake Windermere

Possibly the most famous of English lakes. This magnificent body of water nestles in the Lake District and attracts millions of visitors every year. What many people don't know is that it is home to char, a fish that has lived continuously in Windermere since the Ice Age.

I knew nothing about char, char fishing or the people who do it. However, by chance, whilst I was working for a living, I had a chance encounter with a businessman who had a company based near Lake Windermere. At the time, I was based in Redhill, Surrey, so quite a distance from the lakes! However, I am nothing if not resourceful and it occurred to me that I could combine a "business trip" to the Lake District with a spot of fishing.

Long story short, my business acquaintance arranged for me to go char fishing on Lake Windermere with one of the few holders of the official fishing permit. The right to fish for char on Windermere is strictly controlled and is normally handed down from father to son. Very rarely are new permits issued. This ensures the lake is not over-fished.

I met my contact in a local Working Mens Club and he jumped in my car and off we went to some boat houses overlooking Windermere. His boat was a long clinker-built rowing boat, almost skiff-like, being sleek and narrow. I was to find out why later. But the biggest surprise was yet to come.

Inside the boat shed, my new friend (I forget his name) reached up and grabbed two very long poles from the rafters. I mean very long. These poles were at least 18' (5.5 metres) in length and heavy. He gave one to me and without much explanation, we walked off towards his boat.

As we got in the boat, I noticed a pair of oars. This thing didn't have an outboard. We were to row up and down Windermere or rather, I was! The long poles had a length of braid (strong fishing line) attached to the end, from which, every 4' or so were strung small metal lures, with a single hook.

Windermere is deep, estimates are 64 metres at its deepest part, so the braid has a total of 10 or 12 lures, taking up a total of 40 to 50 feet when dropped into the water. The poles are shipped out and supported by wooden arms protruding from the boat. A lead weight ensures the lures stay deep in the water and as the rower begins to row, the lures are dragged behind the boat on either side. Such is the "drag" caused by this method that rowing is quite arduous, particularly in the face of the wind!

When a fish takes a lure, the end of the pole shakes and rather than haul in the whole contraption, a "lazy line" is tied to the top of the braid, near the end of the pole and this is used to haul the lures in until the fish is found, unhooked and the process starts again.

This method of fishing is unique to Windermere and I am honoured to not only have witnessed it but to also have taken part in catching these rare fish from Lake Windermere.

# Part 3

# Chapter 10
# In Pursuit of Barbel

I have no doubt that there are many small groups of friends and acquaintances that pursue a shared love of a hobby or pastime. I would also agree that these groups meet regularly to partake in their interest.

The group of friends that I am involved with have taken an annual one-week fishing trip in the UK for the last 40 years to fish for the most powerful of river coarse fish; the barbel (Barbus barbus) Its name is derived from the four whisker-like protrusions located at the corners of the fish's mouth. They live in fast-flowing rivers and are second only to the salmon when putting up a powerful scrap when hooked.

Our group has fished for these magnificent creatures in a variety of rivers including the Hampshire Avon, the Teme, the Severn, the Stour at Throop, to name a few. Our favourite location and the river we have fished for the last 15 years is the River Wye in the glorious Golden Valley in Herefordshire.

When we started our quest to pursue these hard-fighting fish in the early 1980s, little did we know that we were in the vanguard of what would become an obsession of many anglers in the UK. Our simple desire was to spend quality time with friends and share our passion for fishing. We had no idea how long this activity would last and if someone had told us, we would still be doing it 40+ years later, we would not have believed it.

## The Hampshire Avon

This is where it started all those years ago. An "advance party" of a couple of my friends decided to fish the Severalls beat on the Hampshire Avon in Ringwood. They returned with tales of large chub and barbel being caught and a wonderful pub, The Fish Inn, right on the banks of the river. It was decided that we all fish it the following year, that year being 1980.

Although we all owned cars or had the use of company cars, we decided to rent a van, which we could load up with all our gear and luggage. I had a contact who ran a vehicle hire business in Brentwood and he kindly did a "mates rates" deal on a blue Ford Transit minibus. It had a huge roof rack which accommodated all our suitcases whilst our fishing gear was stacked inside between the seats. Looking back on that occasion, I shudder to think how overloaded it must have been.

So it was that a group of young men turned up at The Copper Kettle B&B in Ringwood. After introducing ourselves to the owner, there was a mad rush upstairs to grab the "best" rooms. Ray decided that Laurie had got the best room and so to teach him a lesson, he picked up Laurie's suitcase and "pretended" to throw it out of the window. The suitcase was unzipped.

Everything fell out onto the pavement below, showering pedestrians with shirts, trousers, pants and socks. A pair of pants got hooked around the metal "Copper Kettle" sign hanging above the entrance. We had been there less than 15 minutes and the owner was not a happy chappy.

But we were there for the fishing and we took the challenge seriously. We had been given exclusive rights to fish the section of the Avon directly opposite The Fish Inn. Andy was working in the city and his boss owned the rights to this beat, which is how we found ourselves one wonderful September day "living the dream", fishing for barbel on the Hampshire Avon.

What we hadn't accounted for was the streamer weed. Our river fishing had been limited to the Chelmer in Essex and maybe the Suffolk Stour. Our equipment wasn't exactly "state-of-the-art" either. I was using a small 9' hollow glass rod made by the Anglian Rod Company. To this was attached the "reel of choice" the Intrepid made by K P Morritt of Cheam, Surrey.

We all understood that Barbel is a strong fighter and accordingly teamed our reels up with a 10lb monofilament line. A simple running rig with a 2.5oz lead or swim-feeder was attached. Hooks were a size 10 and the bait was a large lump of luncheon meat.

Remarkably, 40 years later, tactics remain virtually unchanged but the equipment has changed out of all recognition, with carbon rods, much-improved reels (with bait-runner options) fluorocarbon line, stronger hooks and hair-rigged baits.

But back to that first outing all those years ago. The spot we chose was just downstream from some small weir gates from where water levels were controlled. It was chosen due to a couple of main factors, namely, it was near to where we parked the minibus and it was opposite the pub. None of us had any idea if this stretch of the river held barbel as we had little experience of "watercraft". This is the art of "reading" a stretch of water to understand where your quarry may be holed up.

In the case of barbel, they like highly oxygenated rivers, ideally with gravel runs and streamer weed and deeper areas, often with snags, such as sunken trees, to hide under. The barbel is a strong fighter and uses the strong current and any hidden snags to great advantage. I have lost many fish to this deadly combination.

Along this stretch of river are several concrete platforms, designed to control water flow and minimise bank erosion. I perched myself on one of these flat concrete blocks and started fishing. It wasn't long before most of us were complaining about the amount of weed coming downstream. We hadn't anticipated the weed cutting that takes place on stretches of the Avon during September and it certainly played havoc with our rods, giving us false bites every few minutes.

After a fruitless morning, we decided to have lunch in the pub. We put the fishing gear in the Transit and thought it easier to leave the mini-bus where it was and walk to the pub. All we had to do was cross a dual-carriageway with cars travelling at 70 mph each way. There was also the crash barrier to hop over at the central reservation.

We successfully managed this obstacle course to get to The Fish Inn. The pub soon became our "pub of choice" as the beer and food was great. We started each lunchtime session with the same, pint of real ale and a packet of crisps while reading the menu. Laurie mentioned that he loved crisps so much he could just eat them instead of a proper meal.

So it was that when our lunch order was taken, we ordered a box containing 2x dozen packets of cheese and onion crisps. Whilst the rest of us tucked into Ploughmans or ham, egg & chips, Laurie was munching his way through 24 packets of crisps.

The beer was good. The company was good. The pub was welcoming and cosy. We all had a bit too much to drink, but this fact only really hit us when we left to get back to the river. The dual carriageway appeared more daunting on the way back. The cars were more numerous and were definitely driving faster. The central reservation barrier was much higher than a few hours ago. How we all made it across the road is a mystery.

It was on this first trip that a pattern developed, namely, a few hours of fishing in the morning. Go to the pub for lunch. Spend more time in the pub than by the river. Return to the river and doze. I have strong memories of glancing downstream and seeing all my mates fast asleep in their chairs, holding their fishing rods and snoring soundly. Later, when moaning about the lack of fish, no-one suggested that our style of angling left much to be desired.

As the years passed, however, we realised that the delights of barbel fishing should never be compromised by falling asleep on the riverbank as every precious moment should be savoured and enjoyed.

We spent many years travelling to the Hampshire Avon and, on one occasion, a couple of non-fishing friends decided to join us. One of them had located an old ambulance which was available for our annual barbel trip. So it was that we loaded up the ambulance with suitcases and fishing tackle and set off for Ringwood.

As we were driving through the outskirts of the New Forest, the engine cut out. We had run out of petrol, but by chance, we were at the top of a small incline with a nice downward slope to a garage about half a mile away. The ambulance coasted into the garage forecourt and we pulled up beside a pump. People must have thought the old ambulance had a really quiet engine.

This particular year our week in Ringwood coincided with the Annual Ringwood Carnival. It was during a particularly riotous evening in a local pub that we were chatting with a guy who was taking part in the Carnival procession. He invited us to join the parade in our old ambulance. We enthusiastically agreed.

So it was that a few days later we lined up behind the Salvation Army band and just in front of the Ladies WI. The procession made its way along the main street and we held out wellie boots and landing nets whilst the crowd chucked coins at us for the various charities being represented. Halfway along the route, a keen-eyed police sergeant waved to us and we pulled over.

'You're not on my list of participants,' he said.

We tried to explain that a guy in a pub said it would be alright for us to join the Carnival.

'What's his name?' asked the sarge.

Of course, none of us could remember his name. So it was that our brief appearance in the Ringwood Carnival came to an end. We happily handed over the money collected and drove the ambulance out of the procession. Great fun whilst it lasted though!

During these trips, we stayed in a variety of places. Every group has different personalities and our group is no different. We are lucky to have an "organiser" as well as comedians, cooks and buffoons! One year, our organiser was in America on business just prior to our trip to Hampshire. Days came and went but not one of us "stepped up to the plate" to organise our accommodation.

It only dawned on us that we had nowhere to stay after lunch on the first day. So it was that we found ourselves trawling through the local newspaper under the heading "Bed & Breakfast". Everywhere was fully booked, particularly when the owners realised we were a group of six anglers, with a seventh joining us when he returned from his American trip.

At last, we had success. We had a telephone conversation with the lady owner of a B&B who had two chalets on the grounds of her house. It sounded ideal. We couldn't believe our luck. Who needs an organiser? We were perfectly capable of organising things ourselves. Or so we thought!

We found the address and the owner took us to the rear of her property. Built on stilts were two large cabins. I was reminded of a TV programme called Tenko which was being aired on the BBC at the time. It was based on female POWs taken prisoners by the Japanese and housed in wooden huts that had seen better days. That was the sight that I beheld that day.

Tired old wooden huts, on stilts, with weatherboarding that needed a lot of TLC. We split up into two groups and climbed the wooden steps into the huts. They were open plan with four single beds up one end and a small kitchen against a wall. There was another small room with a toilet and washbasin. The whole place smelt damp.

Our initial excitement of finding a place evaporated as we realised this was not ideal accommodation and maybe we DID need an organiser!

However, it was near the river and not far from The Fish Inn. We decided to make the most of it. Breakfast was served in the conservatory of the house and was quite good. The owner did have some funny ways though. We were rationed to one toilet roll per cabin and when we asked for another as we were getting towards the end of the roll, she said, 'Another one? What on earth are you doing with them?'

We declined to give her details.

After two days, our "organiser" arrived back from America and drove straight down to Ringwood. He didn't look too good but put it down to jet lag. It wasn't jet lag. It was food poisoning, probably picked up from in-flight food. The poor guy spent two days in a damp bed, rushing back and forwards to the loo and getting through dozens of toilet rolls!

We left it to him to keep begging for more from the owner. We could, of course, have bought our own toilet rolls but as one of the guys said, 'They should be included in the cost!'

So each day we dressed in damp clothes, had our breakfast, begged for toilet rolls and then went fishing. We now understood the ways of the lovely River Avon and were becoming more successful at our barbel fishing. We started to experiment with baits. Luncheon meat was still the bait of choice but cheese paste, sweetcorn and worm.

At this time, around the early-mid '80s, Kevin Maddocks (a famous angler of that era) had invented the "hair-rig". Until this time, it was always thought that a hook should be either buried deeply in a bait so just the tip was showing or in the case of maggots and worms the hook should be more exposed.

The hair-rig confounded the experts of the time. It allowed bigger baits to be attached to the hook by way of a very short length of line, the "hair". The hook was totally exposed. Many anglers at the time thought this method foolish, as surely the fish would see the hook and shy away from the bait. Amazingly, the opposite was true. Fish readily took large baits attached in this way and the hook invariably became successfully lodged in the fish's lip. The "hair-rig" is now an accepted part of fishing rigs.

Luncheon meat was found to be ideal for hair-rigging. We began to understand about where the fish would be and how to present the baits to them. The streamer weed in this stretch of the Avon was quite extensive and the trick was to roll the bait under the weed where the barbel and chub often hide. Getting between the weed wasn't easy but by using a smaller ledger weight, we used the river current to roll the bait under the weed.

When a barbel takes the bait, they take it hard. I once lost a lovely Shimano rod and reel into the depths of the River Wye when a barbel ripped them out of my rod rest with such speed and ferocity that I couldn't retrieve it in time. In those early Avon days we tended to "touch ledger" and as such held our rods all the time (even when dozing after lunch) Barbel anglers refer to the "three-foot twitch", which describes the massive bite indication on the tip of the rod.

My first experience of this was whilst I was sitting on one of the concrete plinths, having cast my bait into a deep hole mid-river and settling onto my chair. I placed the rod into the rest and held the rod butt firmly.

I adopted my usual fishing pose, somewhere between daydreaming and watching the wildlife. After a short while, the rod swung around. The "three-foot twitch". The line straightened and I felt a heavy weight on the end. *Weed*, I thought to myself. I stood up, cursing the weed-cutting that always seemed to take place whenever we fished the Avon in September.

In an attempt to rid myself of this lump of streamer weed, I began to shake the rod. Having failed to shake the weed off, I walked backwards, tugging the line in the hope that this action would strip the weed off the hook. As I was walking backwards the rod suddenly lurched forward and despite my best efforts to shake the fish off in the mistaken belief it was weed, I was now in a battle with an Avon barbel.

'Baldy's hooked a big fish,' shouted one of my mates and with that I had about four guys standing in front of me pushing me further back on the concrete plinth, peering into the river to catch sight of it. At one point, I had to hold the rod above my head to stop the line from catching around one of them!

Finally, the fish surfaced. It weighed just over 8lbs. Since that memorable day, I have caught many barbel and still feel great excitement when playing with one of these magnificent fish. I have learnt, over the years, that these wonderful creatures require respect and care. When they are brought to the net they should never be lifted straight out of the water. They fight so hard that they have nothing else to give and so they need to be kept in the landing net whilst they regain their strength.

Then and only then should they be lifted from their watery world onto an unhooking mat and the hook removed and, if required, swiftly weighed and photographed. They are then carefully placed back into the landing net and re-introduced into the river and only when their strength is fully returned can they be released.

So, having caught my biggest barbel to date, I was in seventh heaven. For the rest of our trip, I was oblivious to difficult fishing conditions, damp accommodation and bargaining for toilet rolls. This is what catching a decent-sized barbel can do to you!

There is a tendency in life for many of us to take the "easy option". In fishing terms, this often means returning to the same lake, pond or stretch of river where you know the fish will be. This proves to be more difficult in river fishing as the fish can, if they desire, travel up and down the river with their progress only halted by manmade obstacles such as locks or weirs.

Having said that there is evidence that fish tend to stay in the same broad area, so if a particular "spot" on a river produces a good catch, there is a high chance that fishing that same "spot" some months later, another good day should result. Match fishermen draw for "pegs" to fish on rivers and inevitably if a "peg" is known to produce big catches, these guys will pray to get that "peg" in a match.

There is a lovely fishing tackle shop in Ringwood snappily called "Ringwood Tackle". It is based alongside the river, near The Fish Inn. We would stock up on tackle whenever in the area. Ray decided to fish with maggots one day and popped into the tackle shop. He took his 1-pint bait box with him and approached the proprietor.

'Half a pint of maggots, please,' asked Ray.

'HALF a pint?' repeated the owner. 'What are you fishing for?'

'Barbel,' answered Ray.

'You'll need more than half a pint, son,' said the owner.

'How much more?' enquired Ray.

'Well,' said the owner, 'the locals normally use two gallons for a day's fishing.'

We fell about laughing. The colour drained from Ray's face! Two gallons! The cost!

I'll give Ray some credit though. He looked the guy straight in the eyes and said, 'It's OK. Half a pint will be just fine!'

In pleasure angling, part of the joy, is that you can wander up and down a river or walk around a lake, fishing where you like. In our case, we were beginning to understand more about the Avon in and around Ringwood. We were also getting to know the pubs better.

A big part of our annual trip was socialising in the evenings. Ringwood in the 1980s had a wealth of great pubs. The Fish Inn was our pub of choice, but there was also a pub in the main square called The White Hart. One evening we decided to eat there and what an evening it turned out to be. Our group has never been overly boisterous, fairly loud perhaps, but never rude or obnoxious.

On this evening, we had eaten well and drank some nice beer and wine. We got chatting with other diners in the restaurant and there was a lovely atmosphere. The landlady and her husband were wonderful. As the evening progressed, inhibitions relaxed and at one point arm wrestling took place with distractions being provided to our guys, courtesy of some local girls.

I have never been on a rugby club tour, but I suspect our evening in that wonderful pub reflected what those tours look like! I am too much of a gentleman to go into any greater detail, but the memories of our evenings in the pubs of Ringwood will live with me forever.

Fishing was the reason for us being there and so it was for the next six years or so. We were comfortable with the area and our knowledge of the River Avon was improving. One year, we even spent a few days fishing the Dorset Stour at Throop. This is another fine river with a good head of barbel and some cracking chub. We also fished the famous "Royalty" stretch of the Avon outside Christchurch.

These were still early days in our barbel fishing experiences. However, our skills were improving and our knowledge of tactics, baits etc was increasing. I have always been aware of the surrounding countryside when fishing, something I picked up from those early days of fishing in Norfolk or the Chelmer in Essex. I have never taken for granted how lucky I am to have an interest that immerses you so much in nature. When fishing rivers like the Avon or the Stour, you are surrounded by meadows and woods. Birdlife abounds.

I have had families of long-tailed tits feeding in trees right next to me and seen peregrine falcons stooping into flocks of birds. But more of that later. For now, I will concentrate on my barbel adventures and the wonderful rivers of England where my mates and I have fished for the last 40 years.

# Chapter 11
# A Change of Scenery

In the mid-80, we took a decision to try a different river. After some research carried out by Pete (Dad), it was decided we should try the River Severn near Bewdley. At this point, I should make it clear that collective memories from a group of, what is, to be fair, old men, are not good. Our past trips are punctuated with various events that become tangled up with incorrect years, places and fish caught. It was not until 2004 that I had the brilliant idea of keeping a "Fisherman's Log" of dates, locations, fish caught, etc. Between 1980 and 2004, it's all guesswork.

Prior to 2004, however, memories have provided me with certain locations. Bewdley being one. This lovely market town sits on the banks of the River Severn and every few years, it sits **in** the Severn. Flooding is a big problem for the inhabitants of Bewdley.

The section of the river we fished had a small ditch running into it. You couldn't see the main river from this ditch, but we all knew where it was. Except for John. As we approached the ditch, we looked at each other and winked.

'Bloody hell,' said Ray, 'the water level is well low.'

'We've come all this way,' I said, 'so we might as well fish it.'

'John,' I continued, 'you might as well grab this first swim and we'll try further along.'

With that, John took off his rucksack and plonked his seat down. He looked crestfallen but surprisingly determined. If anyone could catch a fish from a drainage ditch, it would be John.

We left him there and a few minutes later we were on the banks of the magnificent Severn. Our beat was upstream and we had heard that there was one particular peg that consistently produced barbel. As we walked along the riverbank, chatting away and wondering how long it would take John to realise he had been done like a kipper, there appeared in the distance, a stile. It followed that whoever got over the stile first would get the best swim. Our pace quickened.

We all had the same thought, but no-one said anything. The stile got nearer and nearer. Our pace got quicker and quicker. With 50 yards to go, all hell broke loose. Someone started to run. So we all started to run. Heavy rucksacks, fishing chairs, rod holdalls all swinging about as we ran and laughed at the same time. With just a few yards to go, Ray flung his rod holdall between my legs. I tripped, but on the way down I grabbed Ray as well.

As we tumbled over, we pulled others down with us, not wanting anyone to get over the stile first. We were a tumbling, falling, laughing, shouting group of "grown" men. As we lay in the long grass crying with laughter, we looked down the riverbank and there, staring back at us, was a guy quietly fishing. The look on his face was one of annoyance and puzzlement.

Whilst this mayhem ensued, John had caught us up, passed us and calmly stepped over the stile to grab the "hot" swim. That is Karma.

The British weather plays a big part in outdoor pursuits, particularly fishing. I have fished in snow, hail, thunderstorms (very dodgy, given that modern rods are made of carbon) and blazing sunshine. On this trip, we did have the full gambit of British weather. After one particularly heavy downpour, we went to the river to find the level very high.

As we trudged through the sodden, muddy field to get to the river, I noticed a particularly muddy area, where, I assumed, cattle had been standing. It was a mixture of slimy mud and cow poo. Pete was the first to attempt to cross this mess. Now when we go fishing, we all take far too much gear. Every year, for 40 years, I have said, 'Next year I'm leaving half of this at home.'

I never do. None of us does. Pete had a huge rucksack on his back. He carried a chair in one hand and in the other he carried a bait bucket, full of ground bait. Over his shoulder was flung a rod holdall, full of rods, an umbrella, bank sticks and a landing net handle. Pete was, by any stretch of the imagination, overloaded.

He walked up to the sticky gooey mud. He had taken just a few tentative steps when the inevitable happened. He slipped over. He slipped over with force. It was spectacular. Mud and cow poo shot out everywhere.

There was, for a few seconds, complete silence. We couldn't believe it. Then it started. Loud, uncontrollable laughter. There we all stood, in my case bent over, as I was laughing so much. Pete lay on his back, the weight of all his gear preventing him from not only getting up but even getting onto all fours. He was like a turtle, stranded upside down.

Now, friends would help a colleague in trouble. True friends, would dump their gear and wade into the mud and haul their stricken mate up and out of the mess. What did we do?

'Quick,' yelled Laurie. 'anyone got a camera?'

So, while Pete struggled to get to his feet, we were all shouting, 'Stay there, Dad, just one more picture.'

Whether it was this trip or another one to the same area makes little difference to the telling of this story. We had booked into a pub but after the first night decided to move. The locals loved the jukebox in the bar and didn't seem to have any homes to go to. At 2 a.m., the music was still blaring out. That and seeing a huge dog bone festering away on the carpet outside our rooms when we arrived, contributed to our decision to leave.

We booked into a B&B where the owner was very obliging. Nothing was too much trouble. Bizarrely, the guy was an obsessive DIY'er who always appeared to be constructing something. We fully expected to return after a day's fishing to find another room had been built.

So, we started to fish on the river from some wooden staging. We placed our rods on the staging and, as is common with barbel fishing, supported the rods so they pointed skyward. This is because it minimises the length of the line in the water and being dragged by the current. Barbel bites are frenetic.

However, occasionally they "mouth" the bait first and these bites are indicated by a "trembling" through the rod tip.

Anticipation mounts as you wait for the pull round. This explanation is important, as it sets the scene for what happened next. The butt end (the end that you hold) of Ray's rod was resting on a loose board. This wooden board ran the full length of the staging.

At the other end of this loose board sat Laurie. It didn't take him long to find out that by carefully moving his foot, he could tap the board and give Ray's rod a slight tremble. We all realised how much fun could be had by him doing this. All of us except Ray, who was blissfully ignorant of what was about to happen.

Laurie gave the board a tap. Ray's rod trembled. Ray sat upright, eyes fixed on the rod tip and his hand hovering over the rod. Another tap on the board and another tremble on the rod tip. Ray was transfixed on his rod tip. The rest of us were desperately trying to stifle a laugh. Laurie decided to give him a stronger bite. The rod bounced up and down. Ray pounced on it and struck.

'Bloody hell,' he exclaimed, 'did you see that?'

'Did you get a bite, mate?' I asked.

'Yes, but I missed it,' he moaned.

So, Ray baited up again and re-cast.

Now, this says something about Ray's tenacity (or stupidity) that this process was repeated many times. The rod trembled, Ray struck and swore. Still no fish. Believing it to be the fault of the hook, he changed his rig. He changed bait. More "bites" followed by more misses.

'I felt it that time,' said Ray.

'I doubt it,' muttered one of the Bens.

I have known these guys all my life and one thing I've learnt is that jokes are wrung dry. They are also repeated. So it was with this episode. We wrung it dry. Ray had any number of "bites" before he realised what was happening. When he did, the language was quite blue. Thank goodness for loose boards. Who would have thought you could have had so much fun with one?

The River Severn continued to attract our attention for many years. We fished several beats and moved along its length from Bewdley to Bridgnorth. Each year we would find suitable accommodation and if we enjoyed ourselves would re-book for the following year.

Our adventures followed a theme. Fishing was always the main purpose of these annual trips but eating out and enjoying a few pints ran a very close second. For many years, we fished the Severn and had a trip back to the Hampshire Avon. Then in 1997, we discovered the stunning, wonderful, magnificent River Wye in Herefordshire.

# Chapter 12
# The River Wye

Volumes have been written about this river and the surrounding countryside. My first view of this wonderful river was in 1997. We had spent a couple of days fishing the Teme and then decided to travel to the Wye. Pete had seen an advert in one of the fishing papers extolling the virtues of the Wye at Bredwardine. We drove in convoy through the streets of Hereford and headed west out of the city.

The housing soon gave way to open countryside. We were heading for a hotel called The Red Lion. We had not booked and in the naïve excitement of a group of keen anglers, we never thought that the place could be fully booked. We travelled for about 12 miles along the A438 before seeing the sign for Bredwardine. Five minutes after turning off the main road, I saw it for the first time.

So many talented writers have written about the Wye. I have several books about this subject. One of them is a Guide Book, known as a Red Book. These were published by Ward Lock. My edition was published in 1930. On page 22 is a black-and-white photograph of the bridge at Bredwardine.

Here I was, 67 years later, looking at that same bridge. It hadn't aged. It was like a monument, frozen in time. We parked our cars and strolled onto the bridge, re-enacting an activity that all anglers undertake at every bridge that spans a river. We donned Polaroid glasses and stared into the swirling waters below. Our aim was to spot fish. Any fish, but barbel and chub would indicate great sport could be had.

Barbel have a tendency to roll when feeding and their flanks, being lighter in colour than their backs, are easily seen. It didn't take us long to spot these flashes in the river. Barbel! I will never forget that first sighting of these wonderful fish. I have fished the Wye every year for 24 years and never tire of it.

We got back in our cars and before too long arrived at the Red Lion Hotel. Built-in the 1600s, this old coaching inn has offered accommodation to travellers for centuries. It's a big draw to anglers as it offers eight miles of bank fishing on the Wye. It appeals to both Game and Coarse anglers. This area is overlooked by the brooding Black Mountains to the west and the Wye runs through an area known as the Golden Valley. It's a magical place and we were smitten.

We parked up in the hotel car park and strolled into the bar. It was lunchtime. It would have been rude not to have had a beer, so we did. We chatted with Mike, the owner and discussed rates inclusive of fishing. Rooms were available as were beats on the river. It seemed like a "done deal", but surprisingly we decided to leave it in abeyance and drive back towards Hereford to see what other accommodation was on offer.

We stopped for petrol and before continuing our journey, we all had a chat about the offer from Mike. We had been taking an annual fishing trip for 17 years and always stayed in B&B's so a hotel with fishing and meals included seemed expensive. However, it was a "package" deal. So, it was decided to take Mike up on his offer. We called him and drove back to The Red Lion. This was a relationship that lasted, unbroken, for 10 years.

Mike was pleased to see us back and, grabbing a bunch of keys, he began to show us the rooms. We were used to sharing and so it was that the "scramble" for the bigger rooms began. Mike began to get the measure of us as we squabbled like children, grabbing keys from his hand to the best rooms or jumping on the beds to "claim" them! In the end, he threw the keys onto the floor with the comment "sort it out yourselves". We grew to love his dry wit and no-nonsense attitude.

The excitement of finally being in the Golden Valley for a week of barbel fishing was palpable. Having hung up our clothes, we decided to drive to the river and walk the beats that we would be allowed to fish.

As is a tradition among the fishing community, you always ask the "locals" how the fishing is. Before we left the Red Lion, we asked Mike, 'How's the fishing?'

His reply was one which (we subsequently discovered) he always gave, 'You should've been here last week.' Not much help then.

So, as we strolled along the banks of the Wye, identifying possible "hot spots" we mused about what Mike had said. Were we too late? Had we missed our chance of a successful week? It turned out we had nothing to worry about. "Last week" always eluded us. We never chose the right week, simply because there never was a "right" week.

It should be remembered that the river Wye is not a commercial fishery. A commercial fishery is one whose primary aim is "customer satisfaction" This is measured in terms of a) the number of fish caught and/or b) the weight of individual fish.

So, an enterprising landowner may dig out a huge pit, fill it with water and then fill it with fish. If it's a sport, that's needed, the choice of fish is normally F1 hybrid carp. They have been bred specifically to put up a fight and having caught a few in my time, it's like having a fish on steroids on the end of your line!

I should mention that I am not against commercial fisheries. Far from it. They offer almost guaranteed catches and as the sport is trying to attract more youngsters, one way to keep their attention is to ensure fish are caught almost "one a chuck".

They are also a great location for Club Matches. I know of commercial fisheries where three keepnets are regularly used and total weights of over 200lbs are achieved. This keeps the match anglers happy. Imagine sitting by a lake and not getting a bite in five hours only to find the winner of the cup (and the sweepstake) weighed in a 4oz roach to walk off with the prize!

So, we have established that the Wye is not a commercial fishery. The fish are not hemmed in. They can swim wherever they wish. But here's the weird thing. They don't wander very far at all. Studies have shown that river fish (apart from the migratory species) tend to stay "local".

The Wye is about 160 miles long and obviously not all the conditions are suitable for barbel. But in those stretches that can support barbel, they tend to be the ones that are born and bred there. They move a short distance and take up residence and their offspring do the same, but they do not charge off for miles up or downstream.

So, we needed to "read the river" and decide where we thought our quarry may decide to live. And having found his lair, tempt him out with a meatball. Or two.

Campbell's meatballs, to be precise. Now this was a new departure for us in terms of fish bait. For years, I had fished with maggots, worms, bread and sweetcorn. My dear old Uncle Corks (he of Norfolk Broads fame) would often fish with stewed wheat and hemp. Bit fiddly for me. I also used sweetcorn and luncheon meat and it was this latter bait that we brought to tempt the barbel. However, as we chatted to an angler already fishing the river, we noted cans of Campbell's meatballs by his side.

'Is that your lunch?' asked my mate.

'Not mine,' came the reply. 'They're for the barbel. They love 'em.'

Now to any non-anglers reading this (and a few anglers that haven't ever caught a barbel), you can imagine the size of a barbels mouth if he can swallow a meatball whole. Our new angling friend went on to tell us that he often uses two and even three meatballs in tandem! The only way this can be achieved is to thread them onto a very long "hair" (as in hair-rigging). The fish looks at this meaty delicacy and sucks the whole lot into his cavernous mouth.

That's the theory, but it was good enough for us. After leaving the river, having made a mental note of where we were to fish the following day, we charged off to the local "corner shop" and bought up his stock of meatballs. I think the shopkeeper tried to sell us spaghetti as well until we explained we were going to chuck his meatballs into the Wye. Not sure he believed us.

So the following day, after a "full English" we dashed off to the riverbank. It was a bit "hit and miss" during those early years. Each swim was designated a name, unique to us. Many swims or "beats" have been given names that have existed for centuries.

Often these names are given by salmon fishermen to known pools or areas where salmon "hole up" whilst waiting for the right conditions to continue their remarkable journey upstream. Wonderful names such as "The Monument", "Old Harp", etc., exist for such locations but we decided to start using our own descriptions.

Hence, it was that our beats were known as "Dead Swan" "Sunken Tree" "Duffers" "Deep Hole" "The Gravels" and a few too crude to list. "Duffers" was so named as it was relatively easy to catch barbel from this swim.

Our first week on the Wye was a roaring success. Not in terms of fish caught, but on our "laughter scale". To us, this was as important as catching fish. What is the point of having a week away with your best mates if you don't have a laugh?

At this point, I should mention that these trips are not, definitely not, a "holiday". In fact, the "h" word is banned in much the same way as the other "H" word is banned amongst thespians. Macbeth is always referred to as the Scottish Play and our "holiday" is always referred to as our annual "trip".

The years passed and the number of incidents during our Red Lion days increased. We used a lovely old Isuzu Trooper in those days. Due to the amount of gear we needed, it was decided that my old wooden trailer should be used to carry the suitcases and our fishing rods could go on the roof with the rest of our tackle crammed into the car along with ourselves.

As we thundered along the M40, I remembered looking out of the rear window to see my trailer literally jumping up and down behind the Trooper. How on earth it survived those trips I will never know. I have that trailer still, parked on my driveway in Norfolk. No longer roadworthy, it is kept purely for our cat who loves to sleep on it in the summer sunshine. I confess that looking at it does bring back wonderful memories.

Sadly, one year the Trooper "died" on us whilst leaving the riverbank. In fact, the clutch **and** gearbox failed. We were stuck. There was nothing for it but to walk back to the hotel. It was already getting dark. None of us had a torch. It was so dark and the country lane so narrows that every now and then we would walk into the hedgerow. As we walked, we chatted to ensure we all stayed together. Then Ray's conversation took on an ominous tone.

'You know there are reports of panthers living here in the wild,' he said.

'Bollocks,' came a reply from the darkness.

'It's true,' he continued. 'They say a couple escaped from a private zoo and they are living in this area.'

Suddenly one of my mates said, 'Ssh, listen. Did you hear that?'

'What?' I asked.

'It was a growling noise. I swear.'

It was as if a starting pistol had been fired. All seven of us started running. We were running blind. We fell into hedgerows. We ran into each other. We were laughing and yelling all at the same time.

'It's the other side of the hedge,' screamed someone.

I don't know how long we ran for but at last, the lane widened out and the moon appeared from behind a cloud. We slowed to a fast walk.

'You stupid bugger, Ray,' said one of my mates.

'Well, I heard something,' he insisted.

By the time we got back to the Red Lion it was late, but being residents we could have a drink and so we all grabbed a pint and went into the snug at the back of the bar to recuperate. Recounting the tale to Mike, he informed us that the "growl" Ray heard was probably one of the many sheep that are in the fields on either side of the lane, having a cough. In all our years fishing the Wye, I have never seen a panther. But, maybe, just maybe, one does exist in the wild countryside.

The Wye is a wide, beautiful monster of a river. Its banks are steep and after rain, treacherous. Fishing from the edges can be fraught with danger. In some parts, the water is 15 feet deep near the edge. If you fell in, you would be very lucky to get out unscathed. We always take care, but accidents happen. One such accident happened to Pete whilst fishing the Red Lion stretch one year.

It was all because of a hat. Pete's wife had bought him a lovely, wide-brimmed fishing hat, for his birthday. It was a fine headpiece. We, of course, took the mickey out of it. I don't think any of us have ever said to each other, 'Oh, what a lovely hat/shirt/pair of trousers,' etc. Comments tend to be 'Why are you wearing THAT?'

So, Pete was fishing a particularly slippery section of the Wye, when a strong gust of wind blew his birthday hat off his head. Being wide brimmed, it trundled along the edge of the river like a frisbee. Pete took off in pursuit and in so doing

147

"twisted" his ankle. How wonderful! We had the joy of seeing him run after his hat AND twisting his ankle, all in a few glorious moments. When fishing is "slow" it helps to have these diversions to fill the minutes.

Now I should point out at this stage that this was the year of an outbreak of "foot and mouth" disease in the farming community. Vehicles were banned from driving across farmland and so we had to park in the lane, which was a good half a mile away. So it was that Pete had to lug all his fishing gear across fields to get back to the car, moaning all the way about his painful sprain.

Fast forward two days. Pete's leg looked rather large and, according to him. "hurt a bit". We were in a pub having a lunchtime pint. Pete was still moaning. The only other people in the boozer were a middle-aged couple. Peter hobbled up to the bar, complaining all the way. In an effort to show compassion, I asked to see his twisted ankle injury. In fairness to Pete, his leg was so swollen he could hardly pull his trouser leg up.

'Mmm,' I said in an attempt at sounding medical, 'Looks nasty.'

The middle-aged lady looked up and said, 'Oh dear, what have you done there?'

'He twisted his ankle a couple of days ago and hasn't stopped moaning since,' I said, adding, 'He's just being wuss.'

The lady came over. She was a retired nurse. She looked worried.

'Your friend needs to go to A&E. Now,' she announced.

There then followed an unseemly argument about who should take him. 'I can't drive him,' said Ray. 'I've already had two pints.'

Everyone quickly cottoned on, all claiming to have had too much to drink. I have never been a fast drinker and was considered to be the most able to take Pete to Hereford Hospital.

So it was that Pete and I found ourselves at the hospital. Pete booked in and, after a short wait was taken to be assessed. After half an hour, a nurse walked into the waiting area and announced in a loud voice, 'I'm looking for the one called Baldy.'

Cheers Pete. You could've told them my proper name!

I was taken to see Pete, who was lying on a bed in a cubicle. A rather serious-looking Senior Nurse was standing next to him. 'Are you Mr Bailey's friend?' she asked.

'Yes,' I replied.

To say I was slightly taken aback by her response was an understatement. She laid into me, explaining that Pete had broken his ankle in three places, needed surgery and should have been brought in when he first had the accident. Whilst she was ticking me off, Pete had a manic grin on his face (I realised afterwards he had been given strong painkillers, which accounted for him looking like someone with a secret joke).

We only had a few days left so it was decided that they would strap his ankle up and he would have to go straight into the hospital when he got back to Essex for corrective surgery.

After a further wait, Pete was pushed out in a wheelchair accompanied by two nurses. As we were loading him into my car (he had to lay across the back seat) I got chatting with the nurses and explained that there were seven of us having a fishing trip at Bredwardine. To my surprise (and delight) the nurses invited us all to a party due to be held that Saturday. Sadly, that was the day we had to leave and I couldn't agree to delay Pete getting medical attention again, just in case I came face to face with the rottweiler Senior Nurse.

The story had a good ending. Pete had his operation and now has several pins in his ankle to remind him of that fateful day he nearly lost his birthday present. Interestingly, the hospital paperwork titled "Cause of Accident" was listed as "hat flew off". A first I would imagine.

To access the river, we used to drive through a farmyard and along a farm track which was bordered on both sides by a high hedge. At the end of this track was a metal five-bar gate. We normally took it in turns to open the gate. The driver of the Trooper NEVER opened the gate himself. The reason was this. The Trooper had headlight washers fitted. They were adjustable and it just so happened that Ray thought it a good idea to adjust them so they squirted water away from the headlights and onto anyone within a few feet of the vehicle. Both sides. Hilarious.

So, whoever had to open the gate KNEW, they were going to get a soaking. The hedge was so near to the vehicle that there was no getting away from the washers. It was all so predictable but we laughed every time one of us got wet as if it was the first time we had witnessed it.

The high-hedged track did cause a more serious problem, however. Now we had always observed the Countryside Code. All of us are respectful of the countryside and observe the rules regarding litter, lighting fires and closing gates.

One morning we drove down the track only to be met with the gate wide open. Not good. Thinking some idiot angler had left it open, we drove through and closed it (no soaking that day!). We fished all day, with some success and late afternoon headed back to the hotel. We went straight to the bar for a drink and recognised the farmer who was raging about something to Mike. We didn't bother listening, being more focused on catching up with each other as to how our day had been.

After a short while Mike yelled across to us, 'Do any of you know about the gate at the end of the track?'

We looked up. 'What about it?' we asked.

The farmer took over the conversation. 'Some twat closed the gate this morning as I was driving my flock of sheep up the lane to put them into the field. I had 100 sheep caught between the high hedges and unable to get through. It was mayhem.' He was incandescent with rage.

We looked at each other and shrugged. We shook our heads, indicating that we knew nothing about the gate being closed. Can I now, all these years later, offer my sincere apologies and say that it was Ray who closed the gate?

Due to the number of years, we frequented The Red Lion, the stories are numerous and, in many cases unrepeatable. Our main aim, however, was not to create memories based on non-fishing activities (although these happened by accident) but to chase the elusive "double-figure" barbel. Mike Taylor would hand out a rather nifty polyester tie with a barbel motif and "The Red Lion" printed on it to anyone who caught a double-figure barbel. A few of us own one of these polyester rarities.

My fish was caught from a swim where there was a particularly deep hole and a fallen tree just upstream from it.

This created the perfect hiding place for a huge fish. Food would be swept down in the current and slowly sink into the deep hole when it reached the tree. Anglers look for these "holding places".

In fact, reading the river or watercraft, as it is sometimes called, is essential to understand where fish are likely to be. I am no expert but this particular swim shouted out "big barbel" to me. I was right. I cast into the hole and it wasn't long before the rod tip swung round (the three-foot twitch) and I was into a big fish.

As with many swims on the Wye, hooking a fish is the easy part, getting a landing net to it is a different matter. I had to contend with a long drop to the water on the very slippery bank and with a 15 foot deep river inches from my tentative grip on terra firma.

At full stretch and after a long fight, I managed to net the fish. Now, one thing all barbel anglers know is that these fish never give up. Pound for pound, they are one of the hardest fighting fish I know. Salmon are renowned for their tenacious fight, but I rank the barbel above them. As such, when a fish is brought to the net, it is never lifted out of the water immediately, but kept in the landing net whilst it and the angler, get their respective breaths back.

So there I was leaning over the river, holding a landing net, at full stretch, with a still quite lively huge barbel thrashing about in it. After a short while, I decided to lift it out and take a good look at this magnificent creature. He didn't disappoint. I instinctively knew it was a double figure fish. The weighing scales confirmed the weight at a 10lb 4oz.

I was fishing alone but photographs were taken and the magical "Bens Honour" code was observed. This code was devised as a way of us all never telling a lie about fish weights when fishing alone. The penalty for lying would be instant dismissal from "The Bens". The toughest penalty known to man.

Double figure fish would fall to several of us over the following years, although in recent years this target has been more difficult to achieve.

We are all nature lovers and treat all the fish we catch with care and respect. We hate to see any animals in distress or injured. Thus, it was that our next adventure happened to feature a swan with a fishing line in its beak.

Tragically, this can happen when anglers do not dispose of line properly or are smashed up by a fish and the hook and line remain in the water and when swans dig about in the weed, they unfortunately get the line stuck in their beaks. We were all fishing together this particular day. Laurie was the first to notice the swan.

'Baldy,' he yelled out to me, 'has that swan got a hook in its beak?'

I took a close look at two swans swimming towards us and could see a fishing line running from its beak.

'Yes,' I replied, adding, 'poor thing. What shall we do about it?'

Now, Laurie is ex-fire service and he was aware that the fire service has many contacts in speciality services. He reckoned that a quick call to the local fire station would result in them contacting "swan rescue" (or a local equivalent) and they could sort it out.

He made the call on his mobile, introducing himself as a retired firefighter and asked if they could get someone out to try and capture the swan and deal with it. Job done, he rung off and we returned to our fishing. The swans stayed nearby and seemed quite chilled.

After ten minutes, we all heard the sound of sirens. They got louder and louder. We were in the middle of nowhere fishing a stretch of the Wye running through a field. There were no houses nearby and the only access was down a quiet, narrow country lane. The sirens were definitely heading our way. We all looked around, expecting to see smoke from perhaps a haystack fire. Nothing. Then horror. Two engines (pumps is the correct term, I believe) came into our field through a farm gate and bounced across the meadow towards us.

'Bloody hell, Laurie,' I said, 'what have you told them?'

Laurie looked puzzled, but to give him credit, he stopped fishing and sauntered towards the lead engine. I saw him in deep conversation with one of the firefighters and pointed to the swans. There were now a dozen blokes tipping out of the fire engines and strolling towards the river. Curiously, there was little activity. Laurie broke off his conversation and came over to me and the rest of the Bens.

'They've called for backup,' he explained.

'Back-up?' said Pete. 'What kind of back-up?'

'The inshore lifeboat,' replied Laurie, who looked slightly shaken by this outcome.

Sure enough, a few moments later a large van with blue lights and sirens going, careered across the field with a bright orange rigid inflatable bouncing about on a trailer behind it.

So, 20 minutes after making the call, we had two fire engines, a large van and a rubber dinghy, complete with about 20 firefighters all standing around in the field.

'Where's the swan then?' asked the lead firefighter.

'I should think it's flown off by now, what with all this commotion,' muttered one of the Bens.

Remarkably, neither swan had flown off. They were serenely floating on the river without a care in the world.

Whilst Laurie pointed out the swan, the "boat crew" started to launch the rigid. It was fitted with a large outboard engine which roared to life. At that, the swans decided to depart. As they took off downstream, the boat followed them, crashing through our swims.

'Well done, Laurie,' said Ray, 'that's buggered up the fishing for the day,' adding, 'let's go to the pub.'

So that's what we did. We packed up our gear and went for a pint, leaving the emergency services to it.

Our humiliation wasn't over though. As we walked into the pub, there were two locals in there drinking at the bar. One of them turned round and said, 'I suppose you're the ones responsible for those fire engines in the bottom field?'

'Ask him,' I said, pointing to Laurie.

With that, we grabbed our drinks and went outside, leaving Laurie to explain about swans, fishing line and the fire service.

We never did find out whether they caught the swan.

The pub that we used at lunch times was a short drive from the river. It was staffed by a mother and daughter team. It was a big pub but we only ever saw a handful of people in there. When ordering sandwiches, we were always told 'there may be a wait as we have lots of lunch orders in.' We never did find out where these mystery diners were sitting!

If the weather was nice, we always sat outside. We were aware of a guy who always seemed to be walking around wearing a blue boiler suit. We assumed he was a handyman.

Curiously, he would always be carrying a piece of wood. Not the same piece of wood. Sometimes, it would be a length of 4x2, sometimes it would be a sheet of plywood but always some kind of wood. He walked around aimlessly (we even saw him inside the pub carrying his wood) but with a sense of determination.

On one of our session lunches, we decided to have a group photo taken. We all sat together at a table outside and the photograph was taken. It wasn't until the photo was studied afterwards that there, in the background, was our friend walking along with his piece of wood. Photographic evidence of the "Mystery Woodman"!

Evening meals tended to be taken at The Red Lion. After a day on the riverbank, it was nice to get back to the hotel, have a quick pint before going to our rooms, having a shower and then coming downstairs into the snug for another beer and then food in the restaurant.

One night, Mike had curry on the menu, which we all decided to have. As a special "treat" for us, he served up authentic Indian desserts afterwards. If you have never had them, let me tell you that they are very very sweet and colourful. They are made from highly refined wheat flour called Maida, saffron, ghee and sugar. Condensed milk is also a regularly used ingredient. Ideal food for diabetics! Let's just say that they are inedible.

Not wishing to upset Mike and leave them uneaten, we hatched a plan to hide them in various places around the restaurant. We tucked them behind curtains, in plant pots, under cushions, in fact any place where we thought they wouldn't be found.

Fast forward to breakfast the next day. As usual, we all met up in the restaurant at 8 a.m. and took our places. Mike welcomed us and took our orders. This normally consisted of 7x full English breakfasts.

Mike returned 10 minutes later with our breakfasts. On every plate was a variety of Indian sweets. No bacon, no sausage, no eggs, just the highly colourful over-sweet Indian desserts. He smiled as he laid them down in front of us adding, 'Your Full English breakfasts will be served up after you finish last night's dinner.'

The other diners enjoyed seeing our discomfort as we tried to eat Indian desserts for breakfast!

For the 10 years that we stayed at The Red Lion, we always managed to book our accommodation in advance but one year we were late in booking and couldn't get rooms for the first couple of nights. Luckily there is a huge B&B in Bredwardine that used to be a former Vicarage. Pete contacted the owners and it was agreed that we could stay there for two nights and we would then move into the hotel.

When we arrived at the B&B, we were amazed at the grandeur of the building. It had a magnificent hallway with a big sweeping staircase leading up to the first floor. We met the owners and completed some registration forms. Ray's eyes drifted onto a picture of an animal which was propped up by the stairs. In an attempt to break the ice and demonstrate his understanding of Fine Art (which is zero by the way), he said to the lady owner 'what a wonderful picture. Did you paint it?'

She turned to see what Ray was looking at and replied in a quizzical tone, 'that's a placemat.'

So started a brief stay at this lovely place, which saw several more amusing incidents.

As is common with us when we go away, there is always a mad dash for the best rooms. In this case, our "rush" was more measured as we were being escorted by the lady owner, although our cases had been left downstairs and so the usual trick of flinging a case on a bed and saying 'this is my bed,' couldn't be done. We were shown each room in turn. Being an old building, the rooms were huge and a couple were inter-connected. One room shared a large built-in wardrobe with another bedroom. We all noticed it. Except for Ray.

Having completed the tour, the lady owner went downstairs whilst we started grabbing rooms. Laurie hatched a plan. He hung behind the rest of us and I saw him disappear into the huge inter-connecting wardrobe. We re-visited each room with Ray opening and closing doors, looking in drawers and generally being nosey.

As he approached the wardrobe, we all guessed what was about to happen. The anticipation was almost too much to bear. As Ray swung open the huge double doors with the remark, 'What's in here then?' Laurie leapt forward and let out a manic scream, 'Aargh!'

I swear that I saw Ray literally levitate. He jumped so high that he nearly bashed his head on the ceiling. It was hilarious. Like many brilliantly funny incidents, everyone knew what was coming except the person who was the target. Ray screamed. Laurie was screaming and we were all crying with laughter. Hoppy fell on the floor he was laughing so much. In fact, Pete had to slap him as he started to worry us when he kept crying with laughter long after the rest of us had stopped.

We had been at the B&B for less than 15 minutes.

# Chapter 13
# A Change of Venue

After 10 years of staying at The Red Lion, we decided on a change of venue. This coincided with me starting a Fishing Log. In fact, I started it in September 2004 with all of us signing the front piece where we agreed that "a barbel is only a barbel if it's over 3lb" It was signed by nine of us. Seven of us still fish together every year.

Sadly, one of our numbers, Ian (Nice Bloke) has passed away. Ian was, quite simply, too good for us. He was so so nice. Another of that original number has given up fishing, thus we are now reduced to seven.

On our drive to the Wye, we would stop for breakfast at a Little Chef ("the" place to stop when driving anywhere in the UK) We always stopped at the one in Burford. The cars would draw up outside and we would pile into the restaurant. Ordering "Olympic Breakfasts" and toast with gallons of tea and coffee, we would then be set up for the day.

After eating our food, we would, one by one, go to the loo and then back to the cars. Ian would be left sitting at the table being glared at by the waitress, in case he too decided to leave without paying. But because he is not called Nice Bloke for nothing, Ian would pay the whole bill. One year, he shelled out almost £100 for breakfasts. Obviously, he received promises of repayment. They never materialised. I feel bad now. Sorry, Ian.

One year, we were all talking about sunglasses. An essential bit of kit when fishing. We were in the car park at The Red Lion, all stood around. Ian asked if we had brought our sunglasses. 'No,' we all replied to a man, 'we've forgotten them.'

'Never mind,' said Nice Bloke. 'I've got a spare pair in my fishing gear. At least one of you can have a pair.'

With that, he opened the boot of his car and started methodically going through all his gear. Whilst his back was turned, we all took our sunglasses out of our pockets (like I said, 'essential kit') and popped them on. 'Found 'em,' said Ian triumphantly.

He swung around to be faced by all of us wearing our sunglasses.

'Sorry, Ian,' said Laurie, 'we found them.'

A nasty trick to play on such a Nice Bloke.

On a personal note, when Ian died, his widow gave us all the opportunity to have some of his fishing gear (he had a vast array of gear). Amongst other things, I decided to have his hook wallet. That wallet goes everywhere with me. When I get it out of my fishing bag, I always say, 'Hi, Ian.' Daft bugger, aren't I?

So, back to our new venue. The Pencraig Hotel. Now I do not have to rely on memory too much. I can now refer to my entry in the Fishing Log, which reads:

'Ben's Trip 2007. 9–14 September. New Venue. Pencraig Hotel, Ross on Wye. Excellent accommodation/food, etc. (note: not sure what the "etc" was?) Fishing was not so good although one swim produced 27 barbel in three days. Ben's present: Baldy, Ray, Pete, Laurie, Andy, John.'

It seems we caught 44 barbel that week but as the majority seemed to be coming from one swim, we decided to try a different section of the river. Once again, we seemed to have invited controversy. We went to a tackle shop and explained that we wanted to try a different beat and the guy sold us Six Day Tickets for a section near Foy footbridge.

When we arrived, the section seemed very short, with only room for two of us. Assuming we had misunderstood the instructions, we continued downstream and found a wonderful beat. The grass was cut. Trees were coppiced. The whole section was obviously well cared for and an angler's delight.

We immediately grabbed a swim each and started fishing. It was a baking hot day. I was fishing next to Laurie.

'Thank goodness for these rip-off trousers,' I said, as I removed the lower half of my trouser legs.

'Same here,' replied Laurie.

The thing was, he didn't have rip-off trouser legs. Instead, he took his trousers off completely and sat in his underpants. I have the photograph to prove it!

After a short while, we heard raised voices. Somebody sounded angry. Laurie put his trousers back on just as Andy walked past and said, 'We're being chucked off.'

I couldn't believe it. We had paid for our tickets so why couldn't we fish? As I packed up my gear and scrambled up the bank, I came face to face with the riparian owner of the land. He was a very nice guy but had called in reinforcements when he realised how many of us were fishing on his land. It was these other guys that were doing most of the shouting.

As we reached the end of his beat, we asked where the boundary was. Sure enough, six of us had been sold tickets for a short section of river that at best could only fish two people. Lesson learned. I'm only grateful that the owner hadn't seen Laurie in his Y-fronts. That would've upset him more than us poaching!

In 2008, we altered our accommodation again. We had always used B&Bs or hotels on these trips. We now decided to go "self-catering". This was a big departure for us as it meant us feeding ourselves and organising a cleaning rota, etc. We have stuck with this format every year since, so we obviously mastered it.

My entry for 2008 reads: 'This year The Bens decided to go self-catering for the first time. Pete had organised fishing along the stretch outside our accommodation, Nethouse Cottage, but on our first full day, we had to fish the Wye at Sheephouse, Nr Winforton. Ben's present: Baldy, Ray, Laurie, Pete, Andy, John.'

We also decided to go a month earlier than normal. We fished from 16 to 21 August. The weather was awful. Cold and wet with strong winds. A typical English summer.

I drove separately to Nethouse. I had moved to Norfolk and took a different route from the other guys. I found the cottage fairly easily, having asked for directions from a local garage. The entrance gate was insignificant and was on a fast section of the road. The cottage couldn't be seen from the road and could easily be missed.

I called the rest of them to say I had arrived (and as such grabbed the best room—you snooze you lose). They were only 15 minutes away and so I went up to the gateway to await their arrival. They were driving in the convoy. Three cars.

After a short while, I noticed Pete's car driving at a speed in my direction. I waved. Pete flashed past, followed by the other two.

*Never mind,* I thought, *they had overshot and will turn round, come back and pull in.* A few minutes later, Pete's car appeared on the horizon, going quite fast. I waved. Pete flashed past in an exact repeat of his previous drive, again followed by the other two vehicles. This could go on forever.

There was a long wait for their return. At last, they appeared on the horizon and I made my presence more noticeable by waving both arms frantically and, to my relief, they screeched to a halt.

'Hello, Baldy,' said Pete from his car window. 'It's a nightmare finding this place.'

I explained that I found it easily by driving slowly and looking out for the gate.

'Never saw the gate,' he replied.

'Hardly surprising when you're flashing past at 70mph,' I uttered.

I took them to the cottage and there was the usual manic scramble for the remaining rooms.

The joy of this location was the river running alongside the cottage. No driving to fish. The problem was the lack of barbel. We did well in terms of chub caught. Chub fall to the same baits and tactics as barbel. We were using luncheon meat and meatballs. 12 x chub were caught but no barbel.

The conditions didn't help. This was mid-August but although it started off ok, the week quickly deteriorated with gale-force winds and heavy rain.

Due to the weather, it was decided to abandon the Wye and see if there was a lake we could fish. We had watched the river rising steadily and bringing with it trees, upturned canoes (a worry) dead sheep (honestly) and even a huge gas cylinder.

We spoke to our contact at the Wye and Usk Foundation, who control vast stretches of the Wye and explained that the river was unfishable. He very kindly offered us tickets to fish a lake. We jumped at the chance as it meant we could get our lines in the water, essential if you want to catch fish.

So it was that we found ourselves at Pant-y-Llyn. Luckily, we all had 4x4's as these were essential to reach the lake. We had been given a map, printed out on A4 paper. I say "a map" it was more like a sketch with a blob of blue on it (the lake) and a dotted line (the track)

The instructions read: 'If you only have a 2WD you are advised to leave the car by the side of the road and walk to the lake.'

It should have added, 'provided you have no underlying medical conditions, are able to walk a mile carrying heavy fishing equipment and have the constitution of a Sherpa.' As I say, luckily we all drove 4x4s.

We had been told by the guy at Wye and Usk that a very famous (celebrity) fisherman had looked at the lake in the past and didn't even fish it, exclaiming, 'there won't be any fish in there. Too high. Too peaty.' With that, he drove away.

So, it was like a "virgin" lake. We were keen to get stuck in. There were no swims as such. We had the whole lake to ourselves. Our tackle was suitable for barbel & chub fishing but could be adapted for other species and we reckoned there could be wild carp in this mountain water.

In the end, we proved the celebrity angler wrong. Three wild carp were caught, two by Pete and one by Andy. All caught on sweetcorn, if I recall. These carp are real scrappers. Get one on the end of your line and you know all about it. Modern commercial fisheries buy a strain of carp called F1's and, as the name implies, they take off like a Formula One car when hooked. The beauty of the ones Pete and Andy caught was that they were "au naturale". In other words, no genetic engineering to make them fight better.

We spent our last day at Nethouse Cottage fishing the river, which had gone down slightly, but it did teach us a couple of things, namely: Self-catering is fun and August can feel like November.

The following year (2009) saw us back at Nethouse but we had reverted to our normal September week.

The weather was mild and overcast. Barbel had begun to populate this stretch of the Wye in numbers and although Pete and Laurie went and tried a different beat called Carrots (as in the vegetable) most of us fished the beat alongside Nethouse.

Chub were there in great numbers and my record book shows 72 fish caught, of which 20 were barbel and the rest chub (five of the barbel were caught at Carrots by Pete).

John sadly contracted shingles and left early. Alan also left the same day. Laurie and Andy left the day after, leaving myself, Ray and Pete to fish the final day and clear up the mess left by the others. I wonder if John really did have shingles!

I am intrigued by my final note in the records book. The book has a fine drawing of a brown trout rising to an artificial fly on the cover with the title "A Fisherman's Log". Not very PC (surely it should be a Fisherpersons Log) but it was published in 1993. Despite the book being designed purely as a log of fish caught, I have entered "there was enough booze to go around but we need more beer on draught and less lagers next year". An interesting insight as to our activities when not bankside!

In 2010, things started to get serious, self-catering-wise. We went in the final week of September to a different location. Still fishing the Wye but stayed in a different house at a place called Kerne Bridge. The property was much larger than Nethouse and afforded us more room, but we each remarked how "spooky" it looked. Our fears were not unfounded as during our stay there, footsteps were heard during the night on two separate occasions. One of the lads described them as being "childlike" Spooky indeed!

This week also delivered a Red Letter Day to me. Anglers talk about such days with enthusiasm. It could be catching the carp of your dreams. Or a 2lb roach. Or several 6lb+ tench from an old estate lake. To be honest, every time I go fishing it's a Red Letter Day, as I just love being alongside water, alone or with friends, quietly watching a float or rod tip.

However, to best describe a day that would be difficult to repeat, catch-wise, needs to have a description hence "Red Letter Day".

Ray and I were fishing in a section called Lower Backney. Ray jumped into the first swim he came to (he's not into walking too far from the car) whilst I sauntered off downstream. After a while, I came to a croin, which is a construction, normally of large boulders that have been placed into the river to create a makeshift jetty.

From this structure, salmon anglers would cast their lines without the risk of getting snagged in bankside vegetation. They are still used by salmon anglers to this day but many of these croins were made many years ago and due to flood waters, when the river is in spate, they tend to get partially washed away.

However, this particular "jetty" was in quite a good condition and as it jutted out into the river, I was tempted to sit on the very end and fish downstream from it.

It was awkward getting comfortable as the rocks used in its construction were of various shapes and sizes and none of them were flat! At one time it probably had a concrete "top" to it, creating a flattish surface, but that had long gone. So I perched on the end and set up my rod. I used a Shimano barbel rod and bait runner reel.

The main line was 10lb breaking strain mono with 8lb leader. I always use barbless hooks (there is no need to use a hook with a barb these days) Using a hair rig, I put a single halibut pellet on the hair and loaded the feeder with ground bait. I cast out into the river, allowing the feeder to swing around and settle just off the main current.

In all forms of fishing, it tends to be part luck, part skill and part river craft, i.e. knowing where the fish is lying. I didn't get a bite, so after 20 minutes, I re-cast. Another 20 minutes went by and still no bites. This happens a lot in fishing. 20 minutes can develop into six hours and you go home without even getting a bite!

This day was different though. I felt confident because I knew my set-up was good and my location was perfect.

Sure enough, my third cast, which was a little further downstream, landed amongst the fish. After being in the water for just a few minutes, the rod swung round violently and the fight was on.

I have to say at this point that I continue to be in awe of the tenacity and fighting strength of barbel. They use the current to their advantage. They hug the river bed and if there is an underwater snag, they will make straight for it. I never "bully" a fish in. Instead, I allow them to run if they want to but always maintain a steady grip on the rod and allow the clutch and rod tip to take the brunt of the powerful surges. These fights really get the adrenaline going.

I finally got the barbel to the net and kept him in the water to allow him to get his breath back. I did the same. I then unhooked him and weighed him. A lovely 8.5lbs Wye barbel. I returned him gently to his watery home and he swam off strongly.

I re-cast and settled back to await another bite. Nothing. I reeled in and re-cast. Still nothing. I began to think that the barbel was a "lone" fish. They normally live in shoals but quite often they will live a fairly solitary life.

But the sun was shining. Kingfishers were dashing up and down the river. Buzzards were calling overhead and dragonflies were flitting about. In such wonderful surroundings, I always think of Gerry's words of wisdom "catching a fish is a bonus".

I reeled in and re-baited my hook, this time putting two pellets on the hair. I glanced up at the river swirling past me and suddenly realised that with the cast that had proved successful, I had aimed towards a river level indicator on the far bank. I replicated that cast. After just a few minutes in the rod rest, my rod swung around again. I was into another barbel.

My day ended with me catching 15 barbel. What was interesting was that I had to cast in exactly the same place every time. A few feet out and I didn't even get a bite. It's my belief that as my feeder hit the water, the current took it and swept it near an underwater snag, such as a sunken tree. Barbel hide under these obstructions and if a morsel of food lands nearby, they will dash out and grab it. I had found, by accident, not watercraft, their hideout.

So, with a big help of luck, I had my Red Letter Day. Those 15 barbel weighed a total of 113lbs, an average of 7.5lbs each.

Ray had got back to the car before me and as I approached him I noticed he had stuffed pieces of tissue in each ear because he knew I would be wittering on about my 15 barbel all the way back to our lodgings. He wasn't wrong!

That week saw a total of 61 barbel caught and 23 chub.

The following year, 2011, saw us on yet another different property. Any angler's dream is to have a property near a river. Better still if that property comes with the rights to fish the river and has outstanding facilities.

This year, all the boxes were ticked. The stretch of river we were to fish is called The Creel and the property that has the rights to this beat is also called The Creel. It is in a small hamlet called Foy. When we arrived at the property, we were met by the bailiff, who showed us the river and gave advice on the best places to fish. The weather was sunny and warm. We all felt as if we had won the lottery.

As the week progressed, it got hotter and hotter. One magical evening, after dinner, we all sat on the terrace drinking wine. It was a cloudless night and very warm. We could have been in the Mediterranean. There is very little light pollution in this part of Herefordshire. No street lights and certainly very few buildings. I forget who saw the first one, but one of the lads yelled out "Shooting star"!

We all glanced up but saw nothing and naturally assumed it was the wine to blame. However, as the evening progressed, we all began to spot them. Whether it was a recognised meteor shower, which you read about from time to time, I'm not sure, but for hours we sat there, looking up to the heavens and yelling out "there's one" every time a shooting star passed overhead.

It was a wonderful evening. It had nothing to do with fishing, but fishing brought us here. It was the common denominator in us all being together, drinking wine, looking up at the stars and enveloped in a warm tropical night. It's not often those evenings occur, so if it happens to you, for goodness' sake appreciate it!

We caught 114 barbel and 26 chub that week and vowed to return the following year.

So it was that in 2012 we found ourselves back at The Creel. Once again the bailiff met us at the property and this time just him and Dad walked the river, leaving the rest of us to unload the cars and sort out the provisions. Thanks, Dad!

By 4 p.m., we were all fishing and five barbel were caught that first evening along with two chub. The following day, we woke up to rain. Rather different from last year. This can make river banks slippery and dangerous and it's advisable to have all your limbs in good working order.

Sadly for Ray, this was not the case. A few weeks before our trip, he was in the loft in his garage and, for some reason best known to himself, decided to exit the loft without the use of a ladder. He says he slipped. Of course, you did Ray. Anyway, his arm connected to the concrete floor, which was rather unforgiving and as a consequence, Ray had his arm in plaster.

Now Ray and I often shared a room as Dad likes to "rotate" who has what room. None of us dare argue with this format or Pete may decide to throw his toys out of the pram and the rest of us would have to make decisions. So, Ray and I are in one room with two single beds. There is an en suite. Now, whether it was the painkillers he was on or just plain forgetfulness, but at about 3 a.m. I was awoken by Ray trying to get into my bed. Now, I've known Ray since the year dot. We grew up together and I love him like a brother (in fact we are "blood" brothers, as previously explained) but the sight of his backside easing itself into my bed was enough!

'What the hell are you doing?' I yelled.

In fairness to Ray, he shot up and started to apologise profusely. 'Sorry, Baldy, I thought it was my bed.'

When we recounted the story the following morning, the rest of the lads said they were locking their bedroom doors for the rest of the trip.

Forgetfulness is something you can't avoid as you get older. We were all in our late 50s, early 60s during this time and short-term memory loss was commonplace. Laurie had forgotten about his landing net and had to go into Hereford and buy another one. The following day, he went fishing and forgot it. He had to walk all the way back to the house to get it. Dad thought that was hilarious until the following day he arrived at the river with a net, but no handle. 'He who laughs last?'

The weather was quite unpredictable this week. Wet weather can have a dramatic effect on the Wye, especially if it rains in the Welsh hills where the river has its source on the eastern slopes of Plynlimon, almost 2,000ft up in mid-Wales (that's just over 600 metres in new money). The river travels for 150 miles before entering the Severn estuary just south of Chepstow.

So, if it rains in Wales, 24 hours later, the Wye changes character. Despite the sunshine on day 4, the river had swollen. It was up a good 5–6 feet and the colour of chocolate. We had, of course, experienced conditions like this in the past, but it takes a while to decide where the fish will be holding up out of the main flow.

We all have brollies with us, but they tend to flap about a lot when rain is combined with strong winds. In a previous chapter, I mentioned the passing of our dear friend and fellow angler Ian "Nice Bloke". As well as being the proud owner of Ian's hook wallet, I also have his "storm poles".

These brilliant bits of kit screw into the canopy of a fishing brolly, via a special fitment and you drive the poles into the ground, so that, in effect, the brolly is secured at three points, the main pole and two further poles. I was the envy of the others. Whilst they all clung onto their brollies to stop them being blown away, I sat under mine serenely fishing away!

Ray, a.k.a. "One Arm" struggled a bit as his ribs were also hurting and we were all in admiration of his determination to stick to fishing despite the conditions. Having said that, it would've been hilarious if he had staggered over in the mud.

So, 2012 was a difficult year, weather-wise. We caught 70 barbel (I have no record of chub caught). Alan caught a large eel though.

Sadly, this was to be our last visit to The Creel. The house was put on the market and the purchasers lived in it rather than rent it out and who can blame them? We did all toy with the idea of chipping in and buying it ourselves but it would probably have stretched our friendships to the limit!

2013 and another property in a place called Harewood End. Big place and well kept. Although a little way from the river, it seems we had found more nice accommodation. Laurie and I have the furthest drive. The route from Norwich is a nightmare. It was made worse by a hold-up on the A11 at Elveden and then finding out the M50 was closed. We left at 10.15 am and got to Harewood End at 3.45 pm. Only stopped for 30 minutes for lunch. The other five arrived after us so their journey wasn't much better.

The weather this year was overcast and quite blustery. This always makes fishing challenging but despite the conditions, we made the most of our days at the river.

Pete battled with his brolly during a sudden storm and it collapsed on him, trapping him inside. Sadly, no-one managed to get any photos.

John "Codger" is becoming more "codgerish". One evening, he came down for dinner wearing a new pair of jeans. We asked him if they had been bought specially for the trip.

'No,' said Codger, 'I've had them a while.'

'So,' we asked, 'you've worn them before.'

'Yep,' he replied.

'John, you're a liar,' said one of the Bens, 'just look at them.'

John had not only left on the size and price label stapled to the waistband but also the long sticky label that goes most of the way down one leg!

I don't think he wanted us to know he had bought a new pair of jeans just to wear on a fishing trip with his mates! Bless him! Not wishing such an event go without us milking it, we decided to cut up an old cardboard box and make price labels out of them. The following evening we all came downstairs wearing half a dozen of these labels attached to our trousers.

A few days into the trip and we were fishing different beats. This is commonplace. It is difficult to get seven anglers on one beat so Dad arranges for us to fish in "pairs" with the odd one tagging onto one of the pairs. Laurie and I had gone off to fish together and the rest of them went to fish beats at Holme Lacey. Ray and Alan decided to fish swim near to each other, but had unknowingly picked a launch site for a school canoe club!

Halfway through the morning, about 30 kids turned up in minibuses with their teachers and proceeded to launch canoes and kayaks in the river where the lads were fishing. To say that messed up the fishing is an understatement!

Alan had an encounter with a salmon. We fish for barbel and chub. We are not salmon anglers. In fact, there are special rules regarding fishing for game fish in the Wye.

However, there are salmon in the river and they are quite feisty fish. They do not feed when they swim upstream to spawn, but they do like to attack things. So it was with Alan. His swim-feeder got stuck in a tree (another poor cast!) and as he pulled it free, it fell into the water and was immediately grabbed by a salmon! The fish obviously decided to attack the halibut pellet and dashed upstream with it in its mouth. Needless to say, it broke Alan's line! He estimated it was at least 15lbs.

Funnily enough, this was to be the first of two salmon that Alan "lost" (although of course, he was not fishing for them).

A few days later, the same thing happened in that a salmon grabbed his bait and took off, breaking the line in the process!

When chatting to a couple of salmon anglers a few days later, they were moaning about the lack of salmon being caught. Ray (rather unkindly) said we were having to "shake them off the hook" as they were becoming a nuisance! Pretty tactless.

The week ended with 93 barbel and 122 chub caught between us.

Because in 2004, I had the foresight to keep a records book of our barbel trips, I don't have to rely on my memory as to fish caught, locations, weather, etc. But, something was changing on the Wye that happened inconspicuously. It had been going on for years. To the occasional visitors like ourselves, all seemed right with the river.

However, the warning signs were there. Nature is a great barometer in telling mankind that things are not as they should be. Salmon were in decline, as were sea trout. Barbel fishing could be very difficult some days. Was it due to otters or some other predators? Sadly, the difficulties suffered by this magnificent river (and being experienced elsewhere in the UK) are the joint problems of pollution and extraction.

Now, you haven't got this far in my storytelling to read about such matters. If you were interested in such things, you would already have joined organisations that are fighting these issues.

Let me just say this: Anglers and all those who enjoy our waterways have to be aware of the damage being done by run-off from farms, pollution caused by sewage being dumped into rivers by water companies and extraction taking place. Anyone who enjoys our waterways needs to write to their MP and get this looked into. Believe me, like Climate Change, if nothing is done then it's goodbye lovely rivers.

So, having got that off my chest, we can roll onto 2014. Staying at Harewood End again. Our trips are normally Saturday to Saturday, making Sundays our first full fishing day.

This year, Pete did really well managing to winkle out 10 barbel from The Creel beat. I did less well. No barbel! But something odd was about to happen as Laurie and I returned to Harewood End. We were the first to return and noticed a French-registered BMW parked in the driveway. No-one around. The house was locked up. The accommodation has quite extensive grounds and we thought the owner of the car could have gone for a wander. We looked everywhere, but still no sign of anyone.

As we approached the car looking for clues, the boot was flung open and out jumped John's brother-in-law, Colin. Now Colin is totally unique. He thinks and does things that we mortals wouldn't even contemplate. He had heard we were staying at this place and although he was living in France at that time he also had a house near to us. He decided to travel over from France to stay at his UK place but pop in to see us as well. But why hide in the boot of his car? 'I wanted to see your faces when I jumped out,' was his explanation.

'How long were you in there for?' asked Laurie.

'Oh, quite a while,' he said without thinking it was strange at all!

So, that evening Colin stayed and had a meal with us before travelling to his destination. Be warned, if you see a French-registered BMW parked up somewhere, Colin could be hiding in the boot!

There is a long-held belief that to catch barbel you need to pre-bait the swim and keep the feed going in, either by the swim-feeder or catapulted pellets. This is because, it is thought, barbel are such prolific feeders that you need to keep them grubbing about looking for food. This trip demolished that theory.

I had never fished near John before. I usually fished with Laurie as we travelled together and it made sense, as all our gear was in the same car. However, on the Tuesday of this trip, John, Laurie and I fished The Creel together and what I witnessed was a revelation. John fished downstream of me. He ended up catching nine barbel and losing as many. He fished a single pellet on the bomb. No swim-feeder. No pre-baiting. No catapulting.

He later confessed to me that he had never used a swim-feeder as he didn't want to overfeed the fish, preferring instead to offer a single 8mm halibut pellet in the hope that the fish would find it. Which they obviously did. He did fire out a few loose offerings with his catapult, but even that amount was fairly spartan.

John continues to confound all the fishing "wisdom" regarding barbel fishing to this day. It doesn't matter whether the river is low or punching through after a period of heavy rain, John fishes with a single pellet and catches! There is a suspicion that he could have been a barbel in a previous life, certainly, his moustache looks uncannily like the barbules you see on barbel. But whatever the reason, he can certainly catch them.

In 2015, we tried yet another self-catering accommodation. These annual trips are a joy. Some of us only meet up at this time of year and despite the passing of 12 months, the banter and jokes pick up from where we left off! By this time we are all grinding towards "old age" and have continued our friendships since childhood. We rarely argue and if we do, we end up laughing. A classic story is when Pete was fishing on one of these trips and wasn't doing particularly well. Cue sarcastic comments.

Some of us went to where he was fishing, which was down a steep bank. We stood at the top, firing halibut pellets at him from our vantage point. He was not happy. We thought we could cheer him up by going down the bank to have a chat, but were met with the now infamous sentence.

'If you come down here, I'm going home.' Pete then added for effect, 'I mean it.'

What was intended as a brutal threat designed to make us feel bad about our treatment of him was met with howls of laughter. Some of us had to lie down as we couldn't stand up because we were laughing so much. The look of someone so enraged and threatening to "go home immediately" was just SO funny. After a few moments, Pete also began to laugh and to this day, if any of us get on our high horse, it always ends up in laughter.

Al didn't attend this year as he was moving house. Poor timing. Despite being a man down, we caught 140 barbel and 40 chub.

In 2016, we found yet another accommodation and one which we have used ever since. It is a large house, complete with its own church (now a games room). It offers ideal facilities in that all the bedrooms have an en suite. It is also centrally located to our various beats on the Wye.

My Fishing Log Book was now becoming more "polished" as not only does it contain vital catch information (captures name, the weight of fish, species of fish, location, weather etc) but anecdotes. These are vital, as they are tended to be "regurgitated" every time we meet up.

Without my record book, we may forget such pearls of wisdom as:

Al wrote in the visitor's book 'great accommodation, wonderful location and fantastic food.' We had to point out that it's self-catering. We cook the food!

Al being told how to get to a certain beat and "look out for the layby on your right as that's where you park" That evening Al was annoyed as he swore blind the layby was on his left. After much questioning, it transpired that he had driven past the layby, turned round and came back, whereupon the layby, was indeed, on his left. It took some explaining though!

Me playing the Nancy Sinatra hit *These Boots are Made for Walking* on my phone, only to turn round and see Laurie dancing in his wellies and underpants. Nothing else. I do worry about that boy.

Ray slightly overcooking our lunchtime rolls. 15 mins required in the oven. Ray forgot about them and took them out after 35 minutes. Charcoal and cheese for lunch that day.

Pete caught a lovely double-figure barbel. Cradling the fish, he knelt down and asked Al to take a photo. It's imperative the fish are returned quickly, so Pete released it before looking at the photo on the phone. Al had got the fish beautifully but cut off Pete's face. It was a photo of a large fish held by a mystery person!

And so it goes on. Every year, more laughs, more memories are created. As I write this, we are all a couple of days away from meeting up for our 40th anniversary. A couple of the Bens have had health issues, but after operations are now fighting fit (as much as you can be in your 70s).

We will laugh and fish and drink and eat together. We will re-tell tales and recount stories from previous trips. We will continue to cement relationships that were created many many years ago. We will take the mickey and act the fool. We will share our news. Most importantly, we will embrace the moment and thank God that we have had each other in our lives. Friendships, you can't beat them, can you?

I have never been a "competitive" angler. Some people enjoy fishing in matches with the total weight caught winning prizes of either money or equipment. For our part, we fish every year to avoid the Booby Prize, which is, as the name suggests, a trophy in the shape of a pair of breasts. Ray won this prize in 2017 after a difficult year for all of us. Heavy rain and flood conditions. A total of 66 barbel were caught, which, given the conditions, was quite good.

2018 was a good year for me. I managed to top the table for the numbers of barbel caught, 18 in all. I fished a new beat with Laurie this year. When information is received regarding directions to a new section of the river, it is imperative to understand the terms used and their actual meaning.

For example:

**Suits 4x4 vehicles:** This means the track is so muddy with massive potholes that it's best if you use a Centurion tank to access the river.

**Wild fishing:** This means there are no swims. You are advised to take a brush cutter with you as the only way to cut down the undergrowth. A JCB would be useful to create a flat area from which to fish.

**Challenging fishing**: You will spend all day fishing without so much as a bite.

**A brisk walk from the car to the river**: A brisk walk, carrying all your gear, which would challenge the SAS. Oxygen is needed upon arrival at the river.

**A popular location**: Popular with canoeists, paddle boarders and wild swimmers. Less popular with fish.

We decided to fish later in the year in 2019. The last few days of September and into October. Flood conditions again. It was decided that we needed to buy a stretch of river so we could fish it any time. Andy had a fool-proof scheme to win £24m on the Euro Millions Lottery. All we had to do was give him £10 each. We didn't win but Andy moved into a new £4m house a few weeks later.

Because we were fishing later in the year, a birthday occurred during our week away. John turned 74. As a special treat, we allowed him an extra 10 minutes in bed before bringing us our early morning tea and biccies. This was certainly Birthday Boy's Year. John caught nine barbel the day before his birthday and on his birthday he caught 6. He later complained that he struggled landing the six fish as "my arm ached so much from the nine I caught the day before". Birthday or not, he was nearly lynched!

John left a day earlier than the rest of us but still managed to catch 19 barbel, whilst Andy caught 21. I ended up with the Booby Prize.

Little did we or the rest of the country, know what was about to hit us. Coronavirus spread across the globe. The lockdown was introduced and it looked like our 2020 trip would have to be cancelled.

However, just in the nick of time, restrictions were lifted and we were able to take our annual fishing trip. Interestingly, fishing was deemed one of the "safest" pastimes during the Covid crisis. Anglers are always AT LEAST two metres away from each other and always in the fresh air.

We all tested ourselves continuously before the trip and promised each other that if we were in contact with anyone showing symptoms, we would isolate ourselves and not go away.

For some time, we have been convinced that John is a reincarnated barbel. This year proved it. Many of us struggled, only two of the guys caught into double figures. John ended up on top with 17 and Laurie got 13. Pete "won" the Booby Prize.

Upon reading my records log, I came across this entry: 'Covid-19 is still a big problem in the UK. Hopefully by the time September 2021 comes around, a vaccine would have been developed and life can return to some kind of normality.' With thanks to the scientists and brave NHS workers and all those in the Care and Public Sectors, life is now at the "new normal" stage, although it will never return to the pre-Covid stage.

We were all grateful to still be able to go fishing together, in September 2021, but what a dreadful week fishing-wise. Just 26 barbel caught (although 121 chub were landed). The Wye is on its knees. Earlier I had a mini-rant about the state of the River Wye. I must make it clear that I do not have an academic background in ecology, the environment or water quality matters. However, I do have qualifications in common sense, observation and gut feeling.

Quite simply, if effluent is pumped into a river, the river will die. If that happens, the surrounding environment will suffer and ultimately so will people. This takes time. The clock started ticking on this, years ago. We have now reached the point that the Wye (and other UK rivers) cannot survive much longer. Why should you or I care?

I won't answer that question, as it should be obvious. Let me just say this. Why should our generation leave future generations with our mess to try and clear up?

September 2022 saw us arrive at our accommodation a day after HM The Queen passed away. We all admired her for her lifetime of duty to her country and all of us.

It took Laurie and me over seven hours to drive there. It's a real slog to get to Herefordshire from Norfolk. Sadly John couldn't join us this year.

Ray's behaviour (which has always been odd) has become more bizarre. On the first night, when I retired to my room I found a candle and a cheese & pickle roll in my bed. Other items, including a log from the log store, were found each night during the week. Ray has always put stones in our shoes which we leave near the front door, but this year he is excelling himself. Ray & Pete always travel together. One morning Ray jumped into Al's car and asked why Pete had changed his mats. Pete explained to Ray that he was sitting in a different vehicle. The explanation was probably due to Ray having injured his back before coming away and he was in great pain, so much so that he couldn't fish one day. I think his painkillers were affecting his behaviour. Although that doesn't explain his behaviour for the last 70 years!

We caught 43 barbel and 127 chub. I was lucky enough to catch a "double figure" barbel weighing in at 10.5lbs.

Laurie appeared to have mastered the technique of sleeping soundly AND being able to catch barbel at the same time this year. He "nodded off" and whilst holding onto his rod managed to hook a barbel, wake up and land it before going back to sleep.

# Chapter 14
# Of This and That

Between the Annual Barbel Trips, there are many days fishing in rivers, lakes and ponds. These tend to be local nowadays. Why travel out of Norfolk when some of the best river fishing in the country can be found here? Sadly, barbel have long disappeared from our local rivers but there are plenty of other species, including some decent pike, which makes winter fishing in the frost and snow more appealing.

I am fortunate enough to own a rowing boat which I keep on my mooring. The dyke leads into a river, which in turn, leads into the Broads system. I take this little boat out and spend many happy hours moored up alongside reeds catching roach, rudd, perch and bream.

This is true "pleasure angling". I do not target big fish, preferring instead to sit in my boat watching the watery world go by. I float fish using a lovely little red-tipped float and, as bait, a single maggot. This is the simplest of methods. It's how I used to fish as a young boy. Some things stand the test of time.

There are no guarantees in fishing. You can never guarantee catching a fish, but a single maggot on a size 16 hook suspended just above the bottom under a lovely little float normally proves successful.

I cannot understand those anglers who moan about "blank" days. By "blank" they mean "no fish". How can any day sat by water be described as "blank"?

I have had many fishing trips that result in zero fish caught, but I see birds, butterflies, moths, insects, animals and big Norfolk skies. I have watched bittern flying across reed beds opposite me before gliding overhead. I watch marsh harriers in their hunt for food and owls quartering pastures looking for a mouse. I've seen swallowtail butterflies flapping their wings like small birds and I've had dragonflies sit on my hand. If I don't catch a fish, how on earth can I describe that as a "blank" day? I think we anglers should re-name it NFC Day (No Fish Caught).

So, what of the future of fishing in the UK? I see very few youngsters fishing these days. I know I'm an old curmudgeon and likely to blame computer games and other distractions. Each generation tends to have its favourite "peer group" pastimes. My mates and I only had the great outdoors. The only indoor activities were board games which, to my mind, should be renamed bored games.

Fishing isn't considered a "cool" thing to do. I fully understand that but I do think youngsters should at least try it, but such is the power of peer group pressure that even if a young boy or girl gives it a go and enjoy it, they would probably be dissuaded from continuing.

It's also a generational thing. My uncle taught me. I tried introducing my two boys to fishing by taking them away to the Wye for some barbel fishing when they were in their teens. It was an unsuccessful trip, which probably explains why neither of them fished. They are both talented musicians though, so at least they pursued something else! So, if parents don't fish, it's unlikely their offspring will give it a go.

Without an injection of young people getting involved in fishing, there is a very real danger of our rivers and waterways becoming unloved. I appreciate that anglers are not the only custodians of such facilities but as has been proven time and time again, if there is a problem with pollution or extraction, it is normally the fishing organisations who raise the issue.

None of us should be naïve enough to believe that commercial concerns will "self-police" their activities, particularly if they can save a few pounds by discharging untreated waste into a river.

There have been attempts by the Environment Agency to encourage young people into fishing and some large tackle shops have had special deals when equipment can be purchased very cheaply. I am not sure how successful these initiatives have been and, of course, there needs to be longevity. By that, I mean that if 5,000 young people take up fishing as a pastime, but after a year only 10 of them continue, then it's been a waste of time.

Angling has to get into your blood. I've mentioned it many times before, **catching a fish is a bonus**. It's everything else that surrounds the act of fishing. It's tramping across a meadow with a mate to try a new stretch of river. It's seeing that bittern. It's sitting among wildflowers. Having a brew outside and a nice bacon butty. Chatting to mates. Not chatting to mates. Being on your own. Reflecting on things. Slowing down.

In recent years, I have taken to buying old fishing books in an attempt to get a feel for what fishing was like in the late

19<sup>th</sup> and early 20<sup>th</sup> centuries. Whilst some of the content has been predictable, there are a few observations which have been a surprise to me. In his book *A Holiday Fisherman*, first published in 1934, the author, Maurice Headlam C.B., C.M.G., wrote in the Preface:

'In that delightful book, A Summer on the Test, Major Hills lays it down that those who have fished for a generation or longer ought to publish their recollections.'

So it is that both Mr Headlam and myself, among many others, decided to do just that! Intriguingly, Chapter 14 of *A Holiday Fisherman* is entitled The Future of Fishing. As was commonplace in books published all those years ago there would often be page titles printed, to indicate the subject matter printed on that particular page.

In Chapter 14, the page titles read "The Threat to Fishermen", "The Dangers of Ignorance", "Pollution: Loss of Water", "Organised Effort". How strange that a book published almost 90 years ago discusses those issues that are in the headlines today.

Earlier, I mentioned the threat of pollution to the magnificent River Wye. It seems that 90 years ago, the threat came from an altogether different direction. Salmon, then quite common in the Wye, were being netted mercilessly by both riparian owners and poachers.

Predictably, fish stocks succumbed to this onslaught and as a result, the netting rights became valueless and the Fisheries Association was able to buy them up. Laws were then introduced that strictly controlled netting rights and fishing for salmon by rod and line. What is laughable is the ignorance displayed by people at that time. So many salmon were being caught along the length of the Wye, that few fish made it through to the headwaters to spawn and thus produce future fish to populate the river.

Perhaps 90 years ago, people were more ignorant. Maybe (although I do not believe this to be the case) they did not understand the life cycle of the salmon. More likely (and this is my belief) people were greedy. They wanted to catch as many salmon as they could sell and pocket the cash.

So what does this glimpse into history tell us about today's issues affecting the Wye and other UK rivers? Well, human greed is still predominant.

Instead of netting, the river is suffering from the combined pressures of pollution and extraction. The Wye Valley has seen an explosion of chicken farms springing up in the vicinity. Chicken poo is discharged into the Wye, killing off oxygenating plants, upon which fish and all other water-dwelling animals, rely. This combined with water being extracted by farmers and water companies has spelt disaster for this once mighty river.

In 90 years' time, when the river may well be "dead" containing no life at all, people may ask, "Surely the authorities should have done something to stop it from happening?" I hope they will refer to Maurice Headlam's book and remark on how the people of today learnt nothing from previous experiences. The comparisons are, of course, plain to see. Human greed.

I recently purchased a book online titled *Fishing in the Norfolk Broads* by Peter Collins, who was an outstanding angler and Broadsman. The book was published in 1967, so considerably younger than *A Holiday Fisherman*.

In this book, Peter Collins lists the Norfolk rivers and Broads, giving an insight as to where to fish and what the likely catch could be. That most famous of Norfolk rivers, the Wensum, gets a good mention. The opening paragraph reads: 'The Wensum, almost throughout its length, is a roach river first and foremost.'

He goes on to write: 'Fine shoals of big fish are to be found almost everywhere and they run to well over the 2lb + mark and many anglers have taken as many as nine of these fish in a single day.'

Oh, dear. What an indictment to the guardianship of our once magnificent rivers. 2lb + roach commonplace just 55 years ago. You would be lucky to catch one of that size in a season. Don't get me wrong, there are groups of people working their socks off to try and stem the flow (literally!) of pollution and extraction. It must be like nailing jelly to the wall.

I don't want to end this book on a negative note. Those of us that enjoy the riverside can look forward to many more years enjoying all that our rivers have to give. But, we must do all we can to preserve our waterways for future generations. It is our DUTY to do that, even if it means making sacrifices.

In this book, I have tried to give my "take" on my angling life. It won't appeal to everyone. A lot of people just won't "get it". But, if you are not already into fishing, do please give it a go. It's not expensive to get going. Tackle shops are great places to start and they love giving advice. There is bound to be a local Angling Club near you, so give them a call. Do your research and if you do take it up—welcome. If you are already an angler, I hope you enjoyed these ramblings and TIGHT LINES!